Y0-AVB-371

ECONOMIC OPPORTUNITIES

IN FREER U.S. TRADE

WITH CANADA

ECONOMIC OPPORTUNITIES

IN FREER U.S. TRADE

WITH CANADA

Edited by
Fredric C. Menz
and
Sarah A. Stevens

State University of New York Press

Published by
State University of New York Press, Albany

© 1991   State University of New York

All rights reserved

Printed in the United States of America

No part of this book may be used or reproduced
in any manner whatsoever without written permission
except in the case of brief quotations embodied in
critical articles and reviews.

For information, address State University of New York
Press, State University Plaza, Albany, N.Y. 12246

Production by Christine Lynch
Marketing by Bernadette LaManna

Library of Congress Cataloging-in-Publication Data

Economic opportunities in freer U.S. trade with Canada / edited by
    Fredric C. Menz and Sarah A. Stevens.
        p.   cm.
    Includes bibliographical references
    ISBN 0-7914-0530-3 (alk. paper) ISBN 0-7914-0531-1 (pbk.)
    1. United States—Foreign economic relations—Canada. 2. Canada-
-Foreign economic relations—United States. 3. International
business enterprises—United States. 4. International business
enterprises—Canada. 5. Canada. Treaties, etc.   United States,
1988 Jan. 2. I. Menz, Fredric C. II. Stevens, Sarah A., 1953–
III. Title: Economic opportunities in freer U.S. trade with Canada.
HF1456.5.C2E36   1991
382'.0973071—dc20

                                                    90–34663

                                                    CIP

10 9 8 7 6 5 4 3 2 1

CONTENTS

FIGURES AND TABLES

PREFACE AND ACKNOWLEDGMENTS

This book has evolved from papers presented by academic experts, government officials, and business executives at a symposium held at Clarkson University in Potsdam, New York, in October 1988. The symposium was organized by the Center for Canadian–U.S. Business Studies at Clarkson University and was titled "Trade and Technology: Economic Opportunities with Freer Trade." The symposium focused on the Canada–U.S. Free Trade Agreement (FTA) and took place just prior to the Canadian election held in November 1988. Prime Minister Brian Mulroney called the election after the FTA initially failed to receive Parliamentary approval. The election campaign was dominated by the issue of free trade with the United States.

The purpose of the symposium was to highlight economic opportunities likely to arise as trade barriers between the United States and Canada are reduced under the Canada–U.S. Free Trade Agreement. Four panels of academic, government, and business experts looked at the economic implications of freer trade between Canada and the United States from different perspectives. Several other distinguished speakers also addressed the significance of the symposium and Canada–U.S. trade issues. Their remarks are included as an appendix to this volume.

We have made a deliberate effort to maintain the book's timeliness, since many of the chapters were written two years ago and the FTA was implemented in January 1989. The editors' introduction, written in January 1990, considers some of the issues arising during the first year's experience with the FTA and includes international trade and investment data through 1988. We have also included a postscript written in December 1990 which reflects nearly two years' experience with the FTA and considers recent events affecting Canadian–U.S. relations.

The symposium and this book have been made possible with the generous support of many individuals and groups. The symposium served as the inaugural event for Dr. Richard H. Gallagher's installation as fourteenth president of Clarkson University. We are indebted to him for his interest and continuing support of this effort. We would also like to thank Frank A. Augsbury, Jr., the Niagara Mohawk Power Corporation, and the Northern Technology Council for their generous financial support. We are particularly grateful to the Canadian Embassy and, in particular, to the Canadian Consulate in Buffalo for their assistance to the Center for Canadian–U.S. Business Studies at Clarkson. Without their continued support, the symposium and this volume would not have been possible.

James Sevigny and Charlene Lambert of the mayor's office in the City of Ottawa played a major role in planning the symposium which lead to this book. Others who played an important role include William Averyt, Richard Beach, J. Richard Bertrand, Jonathan Doh, Steven Hychka, Richard Johnson, Eugene Kaczka, Richard Lipsey, R. Thomas Williamson, and Robert Wood. We are indebted to Susan Hychka for editorial assistance in preparing the manuscript for publication, to Susan Amrhein, Renee DeLaporte, Albert Kanters, and William McEvily for research assistance, and to Karen Pcolar and Anita Sampier for tireless and expert secretarial support. We are also grateful to Christine Lynch of the State University of New York Press for editorial advice and her efforts in coordinating production of the final product.

Fredric C. Menz
Sarah A. Stevens

RICHARD G. LIPSEY _____

FOREWORD

Thoughts on the Canada–U.S. Free Trade Agreement

INTRODUCTION

The papers that comprise this volume were presented at a conference that took place after the text of the Canada–U.S. Free Trade Agreement (FTA) was published but before final ratification had occurred. I am writing seven months after the first round of tariff reductions in January 1989. Fortunately, the perspective of the speakers at the conference was such that most of what was said is still of interest, whereas many conferences about the FTA concentrated on immediate concerns and controversies, so that their reports have only historical interest now that the agreement is entering into the routine of slow, but inevitable, process of implementation. Surveying the FTA from the perspective of late 1989, I wish to offer some observations on three sets of questions:
- How does the agreement currently look when viewed from various geographical perspectives?
- How do past controversies and misgivings look from the present perspective?
- How will the agreement look 5 or 10 years down the line?

GEOGRAPHICAL PERSPECTIVES ON THE AGREEMENT

From the world's point of view—no matter how much this viewpoint may upset Canadian critics—the FTA is mainly seen as a natural extension of free trade to a single homogeneous trading area. Economically, Canada and the United States are seen by most of the rest of the world as one unit, so that a free trade agreement between the two countries seems as natural as does free trade among American states or the various parts of the British Isles: England, Wales, Scotland, and Ireland. This is why the General Agreement on Tarriffs and Trade (GATT) members never saw the Canada–U.S. agreement as a

1

threat to the multinational trading system in the way they would view the growth of regional free trade between much more "different" economies, such as the United States and Japan. It is not easy to explain this perceived difference between a Canada–U.S. agreement and other potential agreements in economic terms.[1] Nonetheless, this is how the rest of the world does seem to view the matter.

At conferences that I have attended since the agreement was published, I find that foreign delegates who have studied the text in detail say that they would welcome a dispute settlement mechanism involving their country and the United States that was anything near as good as the FTA's. The bilateral review of disputed unilateral decisions on antidumping and countervail is thought by them to be valuable in giving some accountability and transparency to decisions involving fair trade laws. The knowledge that such decisions were subject to review might even, it is believed, alter some of the decisions that might otherwise have been made on political grounds.

The provisions for services and easy temporary entry of business and professional personnel are also attractive to other countries, as is the curtailment of various measures that can act as nontariff barriers. In particular, the elimination of quantitative restrictions, the restraint on emergency relief from import surges and the constrained use of national defense as a reason for restricting imports are all very attractive to foreign governments, particularly those of the newly industrialized economies.

What impact the Canada–U.S. Free Trade Agreement will have on the Uruguay Round of the GATT negotiations is not easy to tell at this stage. Nor will it ever be easy, since its influence will probably be of a generalized sort, some of which may work through an unconscious demonstration effect. What is clear is that failure of either the negotiations or the ratification process would have had a significant negative effect. Many people would have reasoned that if the United States could not reach an accommodation with the country that is simultaneously its closest neighbor, its largest customer, and its most similar social and economic counterpart, then the hope must be small for the rest of the world. This might have significantly weakened the resolve to make the current round of the multilateral negotiations work.

More specifically, Canada negotiated strenuously for categorizing subsidies into the three classes discussed more fully later in this paper: unacceptable, and hence immediately countervailable; actionable, where, as in the status quo, one can try them on and see what happens; and acceptable, exempt from countervail actions. Although the United States would not agree to this framework during the bilateral negotiations, they seem more agreeable to this classification in the GATT negotiations on subsidies and countervail. It is just possible that the bilateral discussions helped to soften U.S. resistance to this proposal to the point that they were willing to accept it in the multilateral negotiations.

From the points of view of the two participating nations, the agreement appears somewhat more dramatic. To the United States, it has a threefold importance. First and foremost, it is an economic agreement concerned with liberalizing trade with the country's largest trading partner. Second, it is a means to making Canada a safer repository for U.S. investment. Third, it is a vehicle for solving a number of trade- and investment-related irritants.

To Canada, the FTA is primarily an expression of national self-confidence. Supporters believe that the country's industries can compete with those in their giant neighbor to the south, no longer needing the protection that less-developed countries provide for their infant industries. Second, it is a natural development to gain tariff-free access to the market of its most important trading partner. Third, it is seen partly as a defensive move to gain some exemption against a feared upsurge of U.S. protectionism. Finally, although Canadian trade policy opposes any tendency for the world to break up into trading blocks, the agreement ensures that, if this were to come to pass, Canada would be inside the walls of fortress North America, rather than being left outside on its own. All of these forces will have significant, if not enormous, impacts on the economies of the two countries. Many of those potential impacts are outlined in the papers that comprise this volume.

From the point of view of particular regions, notably those close to the border—which includes most of Canada and a significant part of the United States—the agreement will have a major impact. Small firms on either side of the border serving local markets have often had to surmount significant barriers when trading into adjacent areas in the other country. For them, the local market area will no longer be divided by an economically artificial line. Instead they will be able to trade within a local market defined by economic rather than by political forces. These effects may be quite significant. Because they concern small firms, they are hard to anticipate before the event and will be hard to measure after it.

From a northeastern point of view, the enormous industrial area on either side of Lakes Ontario and Erie, which includes Michigan, New York, and Ohio on the U.S. side and the southern parts of Quebec and Ontario on the Canadian side, will be united into a single trading region, with a more efficient allocation of resources within it. Henceforth, economic forces will determine the location of industry and the flows of trade within the area (although flows of labor will continue to be constrained by immigration policies).

Past Controversies and Misgivings

Intense controversies, like old soldiers, have a way of just fading away rather than being terminated by some dramatic judgment, such as is rendered in a courtroom. Virtually all of the controversy and misgivings were on the Canadian side, so this section deals mainly with Canada. The discussion should, however, be of interest to Americans who seek to understand and evaluate the intensity of emotion on the Canadian side in reference to the agreement. Four areas in particular proved highly controversial in the Canadian context.

One group of Canadian opponents feared that the economy just could not stand up to American competition, and that where it could, the costs of adjustment would place a heavy burden on workers and firms. Supporters pointed in vain to the low adjustment costs in most other successful economic unions, as well as to the fact that tariffs on trade between Canada and the United States had been greatly reduced through successive rounds of GATT tariff reductions without the adjustments attracting any significant notice, let alone becoming a source of serious disruption. Supporters also drew attention to the fact that most of the adjustment to tariff cuts among advanced countries in today's world of product differentiation is intraindustry rather than between industries.

There is no doubt in my mind that the supporters were right in this case. It would be truly amazing if the two economies responded very differently to the removal of the last of the tariffs between them than they did to the earlier removal of most of the tariffs. The only new evidence that we have since the agreement took effect is that calls are already being heard to accelerate the tariff cuts. Numerous private sector proposals for eliminating in early 1990 tariffs currently scheduled for phase-out over five or ten years are currently before the two governments. The full set of proposals, some of which will no doubt be rejected, covers close to half of the volume of trade currently subject to tariffs. This follows the experience in other tariff-reducing regional agreements. Once firms come to accept that the tariff removal is inevitable, many would prefer to get through the transition as quickly as possible, thus removing the uncertainty of how the adjustment would play out over a decade.

Critics will never be convinced, and just about every plant closing or merger of a Canadian and a foreign company will be blamed on the FTA, as has been done already with events that are manifestly unrelated to the agreement.[2] The rhetoric and quoting of spurious evidence will continue for a long time. Such criticism will no doubt slowly fade away as the dreadful date of January 1989 fades into the more and more distant past, while the Canadian economy continues to function more or less as well as it has in the past.

A second controversial issue centered on the FTA's energy provisions. Critics, mainly in the oil-consuming provinces, argued that the agreement was a sellout of Canadian energy resources. It was in fact just what the producing provinces needed and what most of them wanted: a guarantee of free trade in energy products. The misrepresentation of the *sharing agreement* contained in Chapter 9 of the FTA was typical of the entire debate. This provision merely made more specific a GATT obligation to share energy supplies in the unlikely event that the government of either country declared an emergency of sufficient magnitude to justify overriding existing commercial agreements. This guarantees that Canada will be a reliable supplier, not turning off the energy tap on grounds of scarcity as occurred in the mid-1970s. Other aspects of the agreement guarantee that the United States will be a reliable customer, not cutting off, or at least reducing, purchases on national defense grounds as is being seriously suggested with respect to supplies from other foreign countries.

Once again, critics will continue to blame more or less everything that happens on the FTA. Currently, oil exploration in Canada is falling off and current supplies of light Canadian crude will not last more than a decade. A running down of Canadian oil exports, whatever the reason, will no doubt be blamed on the agreement by arguing that it has caused a too-rapid exploitation of Canadian oil resources.

It is remarkable how much faith the critics have in the government's willingness to reduce production of dwindling energy supplies in order to preserve some for the future (usually on dubious economic grounds). In fact, the evidence is that governments are more inclined to subsidize current production, thus extracting the energy faster than economic considerations would dictate. The current Canadian push to subsidize the production of offshore oil in Newfoundland is a case in point. This resource, which would be truly valuable at some time in the future when the price of oil had reached $25 or so per barrel, is to be extracted at a time when it will not even pay for the full cost of its development and extraction. If ever there were a case of the future being despoiled for the benefit of some in the present, it is the Canadian government's current oil policy.

A third issue involved investment review. Critics of the FTA focused on provisions to raise the exemption for review of U.S. takeovers of Canadian firms from the $5 to $150 million size, calling this a sellout to foreign business. Yet globalization of business is likely to lead to more and more integration of local firms into transnational networks. With or without the FTA, review of foreign takeovers is unlikely to be a major objective of Canadian governments, who will more and more be concerned with creating units large enough to compete globally.

At the time the FTA was being negotiated, the United States had no restrictions on foreign investment. Canadian supporters of the agreement argued, however, that it would protect Canadian investment in the United States from any future upsurge of American anti-foreign investment sentiment. Writing soon after the agreement had been signed, Robert York and I said the following:[3]

> At the moment, the United States has no rules that discriminate generally against foreign investment—although it does discriminate in specific sectors such as radio and TV. If it were to establish such rules after January 1, 1989, it would have to exempt Canada by virtue of the [national-treatment-of-investment provisions in the] Agreement . . . (page 86). [The stock of Canadian] investment in the United States is increasing about three times as fast as is the stock of U.S. investment in Canada. It is, therefore, in Canada's own interest to get rules of national treatment installed before there is any backlash against the rapidly growing stock of foreign investment in the United States. A decade from now, this achievement may turn out to have been one of the most farsighted measures in the whole Agreement (pages 88–89).

Since the above passage was written, the predicted back-lash to foreign investment in the United States has become evi-dent. The chosen route appeals to considerations of "national security"—a broader concept than national defense. The U.S. Omnibus Trade and Competitiveness Act of 1988 (Section 5021) gives the President of the United States authority to investigate and prohibit mergers, acquisitions, or takeovers that threaten to impair national security, defined to include the capability and capacity of domestic industries and com-mercial activities needed for national defense and security. The passage of the Omnibus Trade Act predates the signing of the FTA and is therefore grandfathered in the agreement, as was all existing investment-restricting legislation that was not explicitly removed under the agreement. The Omnibus Trade Act was, however, passed at a time during which there was a gentlemen's agreement between the two sides not to legislate further restrictions on bilateral trade and investment. Further-more, the toughening of the procedures against foreign invest-ment is likely to take place through wholly new administrative interpretations of the Omnibus Trade Act—interpretations not in existence when the bilateral agreement was signed. Current-ly, anti-foreign investment sentiment in the United States is directed primarily against offshore countries. Whether Canadi-an investments will be immune from the restrictions that now seem inevitable may become a serious point of contention over the next several years. The magnitude of Canada's stake in the U.S. investment picture means that a potential source of con-siderable friction lies in a conflict between future anti-foreign investment procedures under the Omnibus Trade Act and the national treatment of investment required under the FTA.

Finally, many Canadians worried that the agreement would compromise their social-spending schemes, such as the govern-ment medical and health programs which bring free medical and hospital care to all Canadians. Nothing in the FTA, howev-er, calls for the alteration of any program of any social service not covered by the agreement.[4] The critics' allegation that the inclusion of management services was the backdoor through which Canadian control of Canadian social services would slip away was so wrong as to be verging on the irresponsible.[5]

More subtle arguments on both sides of the border turned on a failure to understand the place of the exchange rate in ensuring international competitiveness. Canadians worried that the high corporate tax burden needed to finance high social spending would raise costs, thus making Canadian exports uncompetitive. Some U.S. businesspersons complained that the high costs of financing social schemes such as medical expenses that had to be borne by U.S. firms, rather than taxpayers, would raise American production costs thus giving Canadian firms an unfair advantage.

Clearly, *both* concerns could not be well founded. Actually, neither was. Both arguments are variants of the belief that high-wage countries cannot trade successfully with low-wage countries. The argument omits the role of exchange rates, as David Ricardo long ago pointed out. This role is easily seen in inflationary situations. If one country's costs rise relative to another's due to more rapid inflation, its exports are threatened with becoming uncompetitive. Instead, however, the exchange rate will change to compensate for the difference in inflation rates. This is why countries with enormously different inflation rates have continued to trade successfully with each other over the years. As it is with inflation, so it is with taxation. If one country levies taxes that raise all business costs and prices, this has the same effects. If the country's exports are made uncompetitive in the first instance, then the exchange rate will change until competitiveness is restored.

All observers who have studied Canada's social-spending programs agree that they are in need of reform if they are to continue to deliver the benefits Canadians expect from them at a cost that taxpayers can bear. Unfortunately, this need to reform social-spending programs will be misinterpreted by the critics of the agreement as being caused by the agreement. There is little that can be done about this, but it will complicate and confuse a task that is going to prove difficult enough in any case without it being used for political purposes to misrepresent the effects of the FTA.

HOW WILL THE AGREEMENT LOOK 5–10 YEARS DOWN THE LINE?

Concerning tariffs, ten years down the line the economies will be fully integrated into a single trading system and there will be no serious proposals to alter this situation. No political party, given the reigns of power—whatever their election rhetoric—will want to turn the clock back. Critics will be voices crying in a policy wilderness.

Within seven years, success or failure of the mandated negotiations on antidumping and subsidies will be known. There is every reason to expect a significant breakthrough with antidumping laws. These are meant to police international trade, and they have no place in a single integrated economy. Australia and New Zealand have removed antidumping laws in their free trade area and there is every reason why Canada and the United States should do the same. Domestic laws that govern unfair pricing, such as the Robinson-Patman amendments to the Clayton Antitrust Act which govern price discrimination in the United States, should then be applied: U.S. laws to both Canadian and U.S. firms selling in the United States and Canadian laws to firms from both countries selling in Canada. Since both countries have used existing antidumping laws as thinly disguised barriers to trade between themselves, removal of these laws should be regarded as a major step towards liberalizing trade.

Some vested interests will oppose this change. These are the interests who are able to manipulate current antidumping laws to turn them into protective devices. Such firms exist on both sides of the border and some of them have significant political power. Free-traders and supporters of the free market should continue to apply pressure to ensure that neither government gives in to these pressures and, instead, that both governments move towards eliminating the application of antidumping laws on trade with each other.

Negotiations designed to reach agreement on a joint subsidy code will, by far, prove to be the most difficult issue. During the negotiations of the FTA, the objective of the Canadian government was to get all subsidies divided into three classes: unacceptable, those that would, if used, call for sanctions without further ado; actionable, those that could be used with risk of countervail actions, as is the case with all subsidies today; and acceptable, those that would not be countervailable. The United States would not accept this framework during the negotiations, but having done so at the eleventh hour of the midterm GATT review in late 1988, there is hope that this framework will become the basis for the bilateral discussions.

The U.S. position has tended to be that, since it is Canada rather than the United States that is worried about countervail, Canada's solution is within its own grasp: stop subsidizing and the problem will disappear. Canada's position has been that the United States also subsidizes, but in more subtle ways than does Canada. Canada also argues that some joint action is needed since countervail threatens Canada much more than it does the United States.

To understand the Canadian concern, consider the position of a firm serving the entire joint market from a location in one of the two countries. If the location is in Canada, most of the production will be exported; if the location is in the United States, most of the production will be sold domestically. Therefore, Canada argues, given equal subsidization and equal recourse to countervailing duties, the threat is much stronger to Canadian-based than to U.S.-based firms. With no solution to the problem, Canada holds that it is placed at an unfair disadvantage: given equal economic attractions and some uncertainty about a risk of countervail, the United States has a substantial margin of advantage over Canada in attracting the location of firms.

If the United States is willing to negotiate seriously, a major Canadian problem will be to persuade the Americans of the extent of American subsidization. Many members of Congress seem genuinely to believe that the United States does not seriously subsidize. Canadian surveys of U.S. practices find very heavy subsidization of many U.S. industries, often at the state and local level.

The major difference between U.S. and Canadian practices is that Canadian subsidies are much more transparent than are those in the United States. The reason is that government presence in the private sector through subsidization and other similar practices is popular in Canada. Canadian governments, therefore, choose subsidies that are obvious and can be pointed to with pride in election campaigns. In the United States, on the other hand, government involvement with the private sector is regarded with greater suspicion. Hence, when political entities in the United States seek to subsidize industry, they tend to use less transparent methods.

It is to be hoped that, with patience and good will, some solution can be worked out. The problem is complex enough that if an adversarial approach is adopted by either party, agreement on the issue will be very hard to reach. If the negotiations fail, the agreement allows for the ultimate sanction of either side giving six months notice to terminate the entire FTA. It seems unlikely that, after most tariffs have been removed, either side would seriously contemplate ending the agreement, or that if the political arm were to contemplate such drastic action, industry would acquiesce. It is more likely that the FTA would be left in place, notwithstanding the failure to agree on a subsidy code. In this case, the dispute settlement mechanism, which was meant to last until an agreement was reached on a subsidy code, will—like so many other "temporary" bodies before it (including the GATT itself)—evolve into a permanent institution.

The negotiations just discussed are mandated by the FTA. Looking further down the line, other negotiations will likely take place once the agreement's tariff cuts are completed. A number of opportunities to go further with free trade were sidestepped, often because of strong political pressure from vested-interest groups. Sooner or later, further attempts may be made to extend free trade to some of these areas. Since both sides gave in to domestic interest groups, there is room for various mutually advantageous packages of give and take to be worked out in the future.

Such a package would have to include some subset of the following main areas. First, there would be concessions to U.S. demands for: (1) some liberalization of trade and investment in the cultural industries, especially in the mass media area, which are currently fully exempt from all provisions of the agreement; (2) some further restriction of Canadian rights to review direct takeovers of firms larger than $150 million in size; and (3) inclusion of all alcoholic beverages in the agreement. Second, there would need to be some concessions to Canadian interests by: (1) inclusion of trucking and (very unlikely) shipping; and (2) extension to cover much more government procurement than the small amount now covered. Third, points of mutual advantage, but subject to resistance from special interests on both sides of the border, including: (1) extension of temporary entry regulations beyond businesspersons and professionals to include artists and some types of blue collar workers; (2) extensions to give further coverage to service industries; and (3) further coverage of agricultural trade in the agreement, particularly in areas where current "supply management" schemes can only be sustained when imports are restricted.

CONCLUSION

Today, the Canada–U.S. Free Trade Agreement is being implemented. It should result in significant gains from increased trade and specialization as tariffs fall over the next ten years. Furthermore, the FTA should significantly reduce the frictions that have in the past sometimes disturbed the basically friendly relations between the two countries. It does so in at least two ways. First, it reduces the scope for policy intervention designed to restrict flows of trade and investment, and, by legitimizing the remaining types of intervention, it makes these less likely to be sources of serious dispute. Second, the bilateral dispute settlement mechanism forces the inevitable, occasional dispute to high-level discussion and then, if necessary, to a binational panel, thus leading to a more rational, and a speedier, resolution than has sometimes been the case with past disputes. Taken as a whole, the agreement is an achievement of which both countries can justly be proud.

EDITORS' INTRODUCTION

The Canada–U.S. Free Trade Agreement in Context

This book examines some of the economic implications of freer trade between Canada and the United States, looking at the issue from several different perspectives. Part I considers global and bilateral trade opportunities within the context of the recently implemented Canada–U.S. Free Trade Agreement (FTA). Part II focuses on regional economic opportunities of freer Canada–U.S. trade within the St. Lawrence River valley geographic area. Part III looks at implications of freer Canada–U.S. trade for individual business firms, with emphasis on the management consulting, engineering, computer software, and telecommunications industries. The book concludes by considering the agreement between Canada and the United States within the context of the Uruguay Round of the GATT negotiations and by discussing future implications.

The intent of this introduction is to provide background information to put the FTA in perspective. The following sections provide information regarding Canada–U.S. trade and investment flows, a historical look at Canada–U.S. trade agreements, an overview of the changes proposed under the new trade agreement, and a discussion of unresolved bilateral trade issues. While we consider some of the major implications of the FTA, we do not attempt to provide a detailed review or assessment of it, as that has been done exceptionally well elsewhere (Lipsey and York, 1988; Schott and Smith, 1988; Smith and Stone, 1988). In a postscript following the appendix, we discuss implementation of the FTA and Canada–U.S. trade through late 1990.

TRADE AND INVESTMENT BETWEEN CANADA AND THE UNITED STATES

Bilateral Merchandise Trade

Even before the FTA was implemented, Canada and the United

13

States were the world's largest bilateral trading partners, exporting and importing approximately $158 billion (U.S.) of goods in 1988. Most Americans are unaware of the magnitude of this relationship, while Canadians hold few illusions about the role of the United States in commercial transactions. To put the matter in perspective, U.S. commodity trade with the entire European Community in 1988 measured about $120 billion, while trade between Japan and the United States totaled $128 billion. While Canada is indeed the United States' largest trading partner, the merchandise trade deficit of the United States with Japan ($52 billion in 1988) far overshadowed its nearly $11 billion trade deficit with Canada (U.S. Department of Commerce, *Survey of Current Business*, May, 1989). Another reason why most Americans are unaware of the magnitude of Canada–U.S. trade is that Japan is the largest individual supplier of merchandise imported into the United States.

Tables 1 and 2 provide an overview of the importance and composition of foreign trade in Canada and the United States. Merchandise exports of the United States to Canada rose from 18 percent of total U.S. exports in 1980 to more than 24 percent of total U.S. exports by the middle of the decade, remaining at about that level through 1988. During the same period, merchandise imports from Canada increased from 17 percent to nearly 19 percent of total U.S. imports. In contrast, exports from Canada to the United States were about 74 percent of total Canadian exports in 1988, up from 62 percent in 1980, while imports from the United States in 1988 represented 69 percent of total Canadian imports.

An even more dramatic difference between the two countries is their respective demands on each other's national output. Over the three-year period from 1986 to 1988, about 19 percent of Canadian gross domestic product (GDP) was exported annually to the United States, while only slightly more than 1 percent of U.S. GDP was exported to Canada annually during the same period.

Currency exchange rate shifts account for much of the increased orientation of Canadian exports to the U.S. market during the 1980s. In the first half of the decade, a weak Canadian dollar relative to the U.S. dollar, together with relatively strong North American currencies vis-a-vis the rest of the industrialized world, meant that Canadian goods enjoyed greater price competitiveness in the United States than in offshore markets. In addition, the strong U.S. recovery from the

1981–82 recession boosted demand for Canadian raw materials and manufactured goods, particularly automobiles, Canada's highest value export. Bilateral intraindustry trade in motor vehicles also helped account for the shift in U.S. exports toward Canada in the mid-1980s.

Throughout the 1980s, the United States consistently ran merchandise trade deficits with Canada. However, the magnitude of these deficits varied greatly, as shown in Table 2. In 1980, the bilateral merchandise deficit amounted to $1.3 billion. The deficit peaked in 1985 at $15.7 billion, again reflecting a stronger U.S. dollar, U.S. recovery from the 1981–82 recession, and a lingering recession in Canada which depressed spending for imports. By 1988, the United States' bilateral merchandise trade deficit with Canada had fallen to $10.9 billion as Canadian import demand responded to domestic economic growth.

The top ten bilateral merchandise exports from each country in 1988 are listed in Table 3. Since World War II, manufactured goods such as producer equipment, consumer goods, and motor vehicles and parts have dominated U.S. exports to Canada, while U.S. imports from Canada have consisted of resource-based raw and semiprocessed materials such as forest products (lumber, wood pulp, and newsprint), petroleum and natural gas, nonferrous ores, and minerals. In the last two decades, automobiles, motor vehicle parts, and other transportation equipment have emerged as important Canadian exports. These trade patterns reflect the significance of intrafirm exchanges, particularly in the major North American automobile companies under the Canadian–U.S. Automotive Products Agreement of 1965. The Auto Pact, as it is commonly known, permits duty-free trade in parts and vehicles, subject to some restrictions. Canada traditionally runs a large surplus on bilateral automobile vehicle trade ($6.8 billion [U.S.] in 1988), which offsets its deficit on automobile parts trade ($4.6 billion [U.S.] in 1988).

Another recent development in bilateral trade is the appearance of telecommunications and related equipment in the list of high-value Canadian exports. Canadian companies have developed product niches in such areas as satellite equipment (for example, Spar's Canadarm on NASA space shuttles) and communication systems (for example, Northern Telecom's digital telephone equipment which services private-branch exchanges). Manufactured goods in 1988 accounted for about 52 percent of Canadian exports to the United States, up from 45 percent in 1970.

Bilateral Services Trade

During the 1980s, the U.S. merchandise trade deficit with Canada was offset by a surplus in services trade (Table 2). The U.S. surplus in services trade averaged about $10 billion annually from 1980 to 1986, but increased significantly beginning in 1987. In 1988, a $14.3 billion surplus in services trade along with a $10.9 billion merchandise trade deficit resulted in a $3.4 billion bilateral current account surplus for the United States.

Table 4 illustrates bilateral services trade in recent years. Trade in services is allocated between nonfactor and factor services. The latter represent investment income from domestic assets employed abroad, while nonfactor services include travel, transportation, business services, and miscellaneous government services. Exports of nonfactor services and receipts of income from U.S. assets held in Canada were $25.5 billion (U.S.) in 1988 and represented 12 percent of total U.S. service exports. Imports of nonfactor services and payments of income on Canadian assets held in the United States equaled $11.2 billion in the same year, or 6 percent of total U.S. imports of services (U.S. Department of Commerce, *Survey of Current Business*, September, 1989).

Several features of bilateral trade in services are noteworthy. Trade in travel and transportation fluctuates noticeably, following business cycles, movements in the exchange rate, and special events (for example, the 1988 Winter Olympics in Calgary). Disaggregating bilateral trade in business services reveals areas of comparative advantage for both countries. For the United States, management and administrative services, research and development, and royalties, patents, and trademarks dominate service exports. While payments generally exceed receipts in Canadian business services trade with the United States, Canada enjoys a (relatively small) surplus in the areas of communications, refining and processing, and commissions. However, investment income favors the United States, which is not surprising given the stock of its financial capital in Canada.

Bilateral Investment Flows

In addition to being the world's largest trading partners, Canada and the United States also share the world's largest reciprocal investment flows. Since the early years of this century, the United States has been the most important source of foreign direct investment entering Canada. Initially, U.S. mining and petroleum companies sought access to Canadian natural resources, while major manufacturing firms established production and distribution facilities in Canada to avoid relatively high Canadian tariffs. This transfer of foreign savings, particularly in the resource extraction industry, supplemented domestic savings in a large, sparsely populated country and facilitated Canadian economic growth. By the mid-1980s, Canada hosted nearly 20 percent of U.S. direct investment abroad and the United States accounted for about 73 precent of the stock of foreign direct investment in Canada.

Table 5 provides data on the stock of bilateral direct investment, showing year-end book values of debt and equity financing received by domestic affiliates from their foreign parents. Forty-five percent of U.S. direct investment in Canada is located in the manufacturing sector, while 21 percent is in the mining and petroleum industries. The largest shares of Canadian direct investment in the United States are in manufacturing (34 percent), banking and finance and insurance (18 percent), and real estate (15 percent).

By the mid-1970s, net inflows of foreign direct investment to Canada began to diminish, while Canadian direct investment abroad began to grow, particularly in the United States. From 1980 to 1988, U.S. direct investment in Canada increased by 40 percent, while Canadian direct investment in the United States rose by 179 percent. Measured by debt and equity financing from foreign sources, Canadian direct investment constituted about 8 percent of total foreign investment in the United States by 1988 (U.S. Department of Commerce, *Survey of Current Business*, August, 1989).[1] The growing presence of Canadian capital in the United States has been attributed to several factors, including closer proximity to consumers in a larger market, productivity differences, local investment incentives, and the availability, skill levels, and relative cost of labor (Rugman, 1987).

Regional Trade

Unique in its location, New York State borders Canada's two most populous provinces. About 65 percent of Canada's gross domestic product (GDP) is generated within Ontario and Quebec. With 36 percent of the nation's population and 41 percent of its GDP, Ontario—particularly Toronto and the "Golden Horseshoe" encircling Lake Ontario—is an industrial heartland. Quebec, by contrast, accounts for 25 percent of Canada's population and produces 24 percent of its GDP. Clearly, the Montreal–Windsor corridor accounts for the vast majority of Canada's manufacturing activity.

Table 6 lists leading commodity exports from Quebec and Ontario and the percent going to the United States. While these provinces share status as Canada's traditional manufacturing center, clear differences characterize the two economies, as reflected in their commodity exports. In 1988, Quebec exported $22.6 billion (Cdn.) worth of goods, with 75 percent destined for the United States. Meanwhile, Ontario shipped three times that amount ($67.4 billion) to foreign countries, with 86 percent going to the United States. Automobiles, trucks, and motor vehicle parts account for about one-half of Ontario exports, reflecting bilateral intrafirm exchanges under the Auto Pact. Ontario accounts for about 90 percent of Canada's automotive exports and 97 percent of its automotive parts imports (Ontario, Minister of Industry, Commerce, and Technology, 1988).

The direction of New York State trade with Quebec and Ontario closely parallels U.S. trade with these two provinces and also reflects the high value of trade in automotive goods. Exports to Ontario represented 75 percent of New York's total exports to Canada in 1988 while exports to Quebec accounted for another 21 percent. Ontario supplied 68 percent of New York's imports from Canada while Quebec accounted for 21 percent. Commodity composition is discussed in some detail in the papers by Gandhi and by McGahey and Doh in this volume.

Many analysts have suggested that the FTA will increase north-south trade within the different regions of North America, diverting Canadian trade from traditional east-west flows (see, for example, the paper by Pettigrew in this volume). However, statistics clearly indicate that significant north-south linkages already exist between Canada and the United States. For example, while close to one-half of the shipments of Ontario manufacturers are within the province, fully 28 percent are exported to foreign countries, mostly to the United States. Only 10.5 percent of Ontario manufacturers' shipments are destined for Quebec and slightly more than the 9.8 percent are bound for the western Canadian provinces (Ontario, Minister of Treasury and Economics, 1987).

As this brief overview of bilateral trade and investment flows suggests, the Canadian and U.S. economies are highly integrated, with extensive cross-border regional activity taking place even prior to implementation of the FTA. The magnitude of this international economic activity has generated bilateral friction, in part, as two sovereign governments seek to defend their interests. The recently implemented trade agreement formalizes the existing economic relationship and imposes new constraints and obligations upon both governments, thereby reducing uncertainty about future government intervention which might restrict international economic activity. The FTA creates a more predictable policy environment which, together with the elimination of remaining tariffs, is essential for further economic specialization and growth.

CANADA–U.S. TRADE AGREEMENTS: HISTORICAL CONTEXT

The idea of freer trade—or reciprocity as it used to be called—has been the subject of negotiations between Canada and the United States for well over one hundred years. The Canadian provinces have depended on foreign trade to provide markets for their abundant natural resources and foreign exchange for their import requirements. In the 1840s, with Britain's repeal of the Corn Laws and its abandonment of mercantilist policies, the provinces began to lose their preferential status in the British market. From time to time since then, a formal preferential trading arrangement with the United States has appealed to several Canadian governments. In particular, economic recessions have generally prompted Canadians to seek closer ties with their neighbor to the south.

The first major step towards freer trade with the United States was the Reciprocity Treaty of 1854 which eliminated tariffs on unprocessed products including fish, cheese, animals, butter, coal, grain, and timber, while retaining national tariffs on manufactured goods. Trade between British North America and the United States increased sharply, but the treaty was abrogated by the United States in 1866, partly as retaliation for higher Canadian tariffs on manufactured goods and for British support of the Confederate states during the U.S. Civil War.

Confederation in 1867 created an east-west preferential trading area by eliminating trade barriers among the Canadian provinces and by creating a central government which aggressively tried to build a national economy. After several unsuccessful attempts by Canada to restore bilateral reciprocity in the 1870s, Sir John A. MacDonald introduced the protectionist National Policy in 1879. The National Policy was a program for economic development consisting of a comprehensive tariff structure to stimulate domestic manufacturing activity, particularly in eastern Canada, and generous subsidies for railroad construction and land settlement to develop primary industries and an agricultural economy on the western prairies. The intent of the National Policy was to build a distinct economic base for Canada in North America, but Canada's geography and market size continued to constrain its economic growth and promote north-south trade. Unrestricted reciprocity between the two nations was proposed as an alternative to the National Policy during the election of 1891 by the Liberals, but MacDonald and the Conservatives narrowly defeated the Liberals in the election and the National Policy remained in place.

Serious discussions between the two countries were held again in 1910, resulting in a reciprocity agreement that was approved by the U.S. Congress in 1911. However, the agreement faced stiff opposition in the Canadian House of Commons and fears of closer economic integration with the United States dominated the ensuing election campaign. The agreement's Liberal Party sponsors, led by Prime Minister Wilfred Laurier, were defeated in the election. Trade liberalization was again the subject of negotiations between Canada and the United States in the mid-1930s, largely in response to high tariffs associated with the Smoot-Hawley Act, which had been passed by the United States in 1930. Significant bilateral tariff reductions were negotiated in 1935 and again in 1938, as both countries came to realize that protectionist trade policies were detrimental to their economic welfare.

The impetus toward freer trade was confirmed again in 1947 when both Canada and the United States became charter members of the General Agreement on Tariffs and Trade (GATT). GATT members meet periodically to negotiate mutually advantageous reductions in tariffs and other barriers to world trade. This multilateral forum has benefited Canada over the years because it reduces the asymmetries of bargaining bilaterally with the United States. The GATT has also served to structure trade relations between the two countries and provides a process by which some types of bilateral trade disputes can be resolved. Nonetheless, Canadian concern about increasing U.S. protectionism, cumbersome GATT procedures, and U.S. preoccupation with third country issues at the GATT led Canada to consider special bilateral arrangements with the United States while it continued to support multilateral trade negotiations (see the paper by Shannon in this volume).

In 1983, Canada and the United States explored the possibility of liberalizing trade on a sectoral basis. Discussions focused on reducing trade barriers in steel, urban transportation equipment, agricultural implements, and traded computer services. The talks ended after one year without agreement when the difficulty of balancing concessions and benefits within the narrow confines of specific sectors became apparent. In 1985, the Canadian government asked the United States to begin comprehensive trade-liberalizing negotiations, and the Canada–U.S. Free Trade Agreement was the outcome of those negotiations. The FTA can be viewed as elaborating the commitments of the two countries to each other under the rules of the GATT while at the same time significantly extending the scope of coverage and the process of dispute resolution. Many observers believe that the agreement's innovations will serve as a model for the current round of GATT negotiations —the Uruguay Round—which is scheduled for completion in 1990 and has focused on the growing worldwide use of nontariff barriers and the need to reform rules for trade in services, intellectual property, and agriculture.

Several papers in this volume discuss factors that prompted the Canada–U.S. free trade negotiations. The negotiations ended with the signing of a preliminary agreement in October 1987 by President Reagan and Prime Minister Mulroney. Enabling legislation to implement the terms of the FTA was approved by the U.S. Congress and signed by President Reagan in the fall of 1988. After being passed by the Canadian House of Commons, the agreement was blocked in the Canadian Senate. Free trade became the dominant issue in the Canadian federal election held in November 1988. The reelection of a Progressive Conservative majority government resulted in approval of implementing legislation by the Canadian Parliament in December 1988, thereby completing the ratification process in the two countries.[2] The FTA was implemented according to schedule on 1 January 1989.

OVERVIEW OF THE CANADA–U.S. FREE TRADE AGREEMENT[3]

The basic objective of the FTA is to further open markets for trade and investment in goods and services between the world's two largest trading partners. The FTA sets up principles and procedures for resolving trade disputes and lowering barriers to trade, ultimately enhancing efficiency, income, and economic growth for both countries. The agreement provides national treatment for a wide range of firms to operate in both countries, meaning that the other party is entitled to the same treatment that each government gives its own nationals. National treatment allows both Canada and the United States to follow their own domestic policies in certain areas (for example, with respect to agriculture and energy), so long as these policies are not used to discriminate solely on the basis of nationality. National treatment provisions apply to goods and, with certain exceptions, to investment and to firms providing services. An important implication of the FTA is that it forces future governments in both countries to be less interventionist in matters of international trade. However, a few major industries are not covered within the FTA, notably beer, transportation, and some cultural enterprises, including publishing, broadcasting, and related communications. As well, only services specifically enumerated in the FTA are covered by the agreement; in addition, intellectual property, a major U.S. concern, is not addressed.

Tariff Removal

It has been estimated that about 75 percent of Canada–U.S. trade was duty free prior to the FTA. Canadian tariffs on dutiable U.S. imports averaged about 9–10 percent, while the average U.S. tariff on Canadian dutiable imports was 3–4 percent. Nevertheless, one of the most important achievements of the FTA is the elimination of virtually all tariffs on merchandise trade between the two countries over a ten-year period ending in January 1998. To be entitled to duty-free treatment, goods must be wholly produced or obtained in either Canada or the United States or must be sufficiently transformed in either or both of the countries so as to be subject to a change in tariff classification. Furthermore, for certain goods such as automobile products, at least 50 percent of the direct cost of manufacturing must be attributable to Canadian or U.S. materials.

Tariffs on some products were eliminated entirely when the FTA was implemented in January 1989, but most will be phased out over five to ten years in equal annual installments, according to a transition schedule designed to minimize employment adjustments in import-sensitive industries. The FTA also allowed the process of tariff elimination to be accelerated by mutual consent. In response to industry petitions, provisional agreement was reached in November 1989 at the second meeting of the Canada–U.S. Trade Commission to accelerate the elimination of tariffs on more than 400 goods.

Canadian and U.S. tariff levels and trade flows for selected commodities in 1988 are shown in Table 7. Tables 8 and 9 show the staging of tariff cuts and dutiable values for major bilateral merchandise trade categories at the two-digit Standard Industrial Classification (SIC) level. Duties were eliminated in January 1989 on about 7 percent of U.S. dutiable imports from Canada and 13 percent of Canadian dutiable imports from the United States. Included in this category were such products as computers and related equipment, motorcycles, leather and fur garments, vending machines, ice skates, and certain kinds of telecommunications equipment.

Tariffs on commodities that account for 58 percent of U.S. dutiable imports from Canada and 34 percent of Canadian dutiable imports from the United States were to be eliminated over a period of five years. This group included paper and paper products, printed matter, paints, furniture, chemicals including resins, after-market automotive parts, precious jewelry, most machinery, petroleum, and subway cars. Tariffs on the remaining 35 percent of U.S. dutiable imports from Canada and 53 percent of Canadian dutiable imports from the United States were to be phased out over a ten-year period. Included in this staging category were plastics, rubber, most wood products, base-metal products, textiles and apparel, footwear, railcars, pleasure craft, steel, watches, and most agricultural and food products. Tariff reduction will be accelerated for many of these commodities as a result of the Canada–U.S. Trade Commission decision in November of 1989. Scheduled to take effect in April 1990, these reductions apply to approximately $3 billion of Canadian exports to the United States and to the same value of U.S. exports to Canada. Goods for which tariff reductions will be accelerated include printed circuit boards, chemicals, electric motors, pharmaceuticals, scientific instruments and other industrial products. In the majority of cases, the tariff was to be eliminated entirely in 1990.[4]

It should be emphasized that before January 1989, tariffs applied to only about 25 percent of Canada–U.S. trade. The impact of tariff cuts on actual trade between the two countries depends on the existing levels of tariffs and volume of trade, the staging of the reductions, the responsiveness of demand to lower import prices, and, ultimately, the effect of the increase in consumers' real incomes, productivity and other economic gains resulting from freer trade between the countries.

Agriculture

Under the FTA, all agricultural tariffs between the two countries will be eliminated over 10 years. Provision is also made to abandon use of export subsidies on bilateral trade and to restrict some nontariff barriers on grains, meat, poultry, eggs, and sugar. However, the FTA does not restrict the ability of either country to maintain their subsidy programs or to legislate changes in their supply management policies. Both countries also recognize that the multilateral GATT negotiations are critical for further liberalization of agricultural trade. By eliminating tariffs, however, the FTA begins to whittle away at agricultural protection, but significant nontariff barriers remain to distort bilateral agricultural trade.

Energy

The United States and Canada share the world's largest bilateral trade in energy products, totaling $10.6 billion (U.S.) in 1988. Most of this trade involves Canadian exports of petroleum, natural gas, electricity, and uranium. Canada itself is the largest export market for U.S. coal. The FTA ensures that Canada–U.S. trade in energy products will be based on commercial considerations, with prices for trading purposes determined by market forces. Each country remains free to pursue its own domestic energy regulatory policies so long as they are not discriminatory against the other country.

The agreement contains broad-based commitments not to impose restrictions—including quotas, export taxes, and minimum price requirements—on Canadian and U.S. exports and imports of energy products. The agreement also prohibits either country from restricting energy exports except during emergencies such as supply shortages or for military-related requirements (a narrower criterion than "national security purposes"). If either country imposes supply restrictions, the other country must be given access to the same proportion of the total domestic supply that it received in the most recent 36-month period prior to the imposition of the restriction. Essentially, the United States has increased its dependence on Canadian energy by ensuring free access to its market. Canada, by accepting this guaranteed access, has pledged to share supplies in times of crisis and not to use government policy to distort prices charged in the two countries.

Automotive Trade

The FTA permits the continued existence of the Auto Pact. Qualified producers will be able to import duty free into Canada from third countries if they meet production and Canadian content requirements in Canada and, with very few exceptions, are original members of the Auto Pact. Bilateral trade in automotive goods and vehicles will be duty free under the FTA as long as at least 50 percent of the direct cost of manufacturing is U.S. or Canadian content. Designed to protect parts producers from offshore competition, this requirement is more stringent than the previous one which permitted inclusion of overhead and other indirect production costs. Canada also agreed to terminate its export-based and production-based duty remission programs. Both programs generated significant U.S. opposition as companies which were not original members of the Auto Pact were able to earn import credits into Canada by exporting to the United States. Canada will also phase out its embargo on imports of used cars. Finally, both countries agreed to establish a binational working group to study the future of the North American automotive industry and to recommend policy changes.

Services

The inclusion of services in an international trade agreement is one of the major accomplishments of the FTA. The agreement extends the principle of national treatment to certain listed services, requiring that regulations governing any covered service not be discriminatory in design. However, the liberalization is limited. While no new discrimination is allowed, the FTA does grandfather existing practices and licensing procedures. These two provisions effectively create a standstill arrangement for policies that restrict cross-border services transactions.

The agreement's provisions apply to services trade in such sectors as agriculture, forestry, construction, real estate, insurance, computers, tourism, and architecture. Not covered by the FTA are transportation, telephone service, child care, legal services, and government-provided services in health, education, and social areas. The principle of national treatment encompasses the production, distribution, and sale of the service; the right to establish a commercial presence in the other country; access to domestic distribution channels; and the investment necessary for providing the service, subject to restrictions on investment discussed in Chapter 16 of the FTA.

Annexes to the services chapter of the FTA provide more detailed treatment for tourism, architecture, and computer-enhanced telecommunications services and begin the process of reducing existing restrictions.

An important provision concerning trade in services prohibits the use of occupational licensing and certification as a barrier to trade and encourages each country to recognize the other's licensing procedures for those who provide covered services. Current discriminatory practices in services are likely to be an issue addressed in future negotiations, along with lengthening the list of services covered by the agreement.

Temporary Entry for Business Persons

Another part of the FTA deals with "temporary entry provisions" for individuals from each country who desire to conduct business in the other country. The new rules streamline on a reciprocal basis the criteria for temporary admission for business purposes and should facilitate both short- and long-term entry, depending on the type of commercial activity involved. The agreement identifies four categories of business travelers: business visitors, professionals, traders and investors, and intracompany transferees. To qualify for temporary entry into either country, business travelers and professionals who satisfy normal health and immigration requirements must simply document that they fall into one of the covered occupations or professions and indicate the nature of their business. The agreement also sets forth less restrictive rules regarding temporary entry for intracompany transferees and traders and investors.

Investment

Chapter 16 of the FTA, with certain exceptions, applies the principle of national treatment to investment laws and policies enacted in the future in both countries. The provisions of this chapter do not apply to investment related to financial services, government procurement, transportation services, or cultural and publishing industries. While not creating a completely open environment for investment, the FTA generally permits investment funds to move across the border more freely than in the past. The national treatment provisions apply only to future laws and practices, thereby grandfathering any existing rules that now discriminate against investment in the two countries. By removing the threat of future investment restrictions in both countries, this chapter is viewed as a major gain for Canada;

alone among other foreign investors, Canada will receive preferential treatment in the United States by being exempt from measures designed to regulate or restrict foreign investment.

Canadian rules for the acquisition of existing businesses will be relaxed by raising the threshold for review of U.S. direct acquisitions of Canadian firms from $5 million to $150 million by 1992.[5] The agreement eliminates altogether Canadian review of indirect acquisitions, which occurs, for example, when the U.S. parent of a Canadian subsidiary is taken over by another U.S. company. The FTA also prohibits new trade-related performance requirements pertaining to local content or the export of a given quantity of production. This feature is particularly important for the United States because past Canadian governments have favored such intervention in the hopes of increasing the benefits of foreign investment in Canada.

Financial Services

The FTA covers all future laws, regulations, and practices relating to financial institutions in both countries. The FTA allows Canadian and U.S. financial firms (including banks, securities firms, and certain parts of insurance companies) to compete on a more equitable basis on both sides of the border and gives them preferential treatment relative to third-country firms operating in either country. The United States agrees to allow domestic and Canadian banks to deal in Canadian government securities, including provincial and crown corporation obligations if fully guaranteed by a Canadian government. Current interstate banking operations of Canadian banks, grandfathered under the International Banking Act of 1978, are protected by the FTA. Should the Glass-Steagall Act be amended in the United States, Canadian banks would receive national treatment. Canada, for its part, effectively exempts the United States from the 25 percent ceiling on nonresident group ownership of individual banks; the 10 percent limit on individual nonresident ownership of federally chartered trusts, insurance companies, and investment companies; and the 16 percent aggregate capital limitation on foreign ownership of Canadian bank assets.

Dispute Settlement

Implementing free trade and resolving bilateral trade disputes are important issues addressed by Chapters 18 and 19 of the FTA. One of Canada's primary objectives in negotiating the FTA was to secure access to the U.S. market which, it believed, was impaired in increasingly arbitrary ways by numerous antidumping and countervailing duty investigations and protectionist pressures building in Congress. In essence, the agreement institutionalizes binational consultative procedures to avoid disputes and to expeditiously resolve issues when trade measures or proposed legislative or regulatory changes in either country threaten to distort bilateral trade and investment. The agreement creates two separate mechanisms for dispute settlement, one dealing primarily with matters of interpreting and implementing the FTA, the other dealing with the contentious issues of antidumping and countervailing duty determinations.

Chapter 18 of the agreement establishes the Canada–U.S. Trade Commission, comprised of cabinet-level appointees from both countries, to oversee the implementation of the FTA and to resolve disputes relating to its interpretation and/or implementation. If disagreements on particular issues cannot be expeditiously settled by consultation, either government can request a meeting of the Commission. The Commission can consult technical advisors; appoint a mutually acceptable mediator; establish a panel of experts to review the issue; or refer the dispute to a five-member binational panel for a recommendation (which may be binding only if both parties agree). If a government fails to comply with the final report of the panel or the Commission is unable to resolve a dispute after receiving the panel's report, the other government may retaliate by withdrawing trading benefits of equivalent effect.

The first panel constituted under Chapter 18 considered a trade dispute involving a Canadian requirement that West Coast salmon and herring be landed and counted in Canada prior to export. The panel's nonbinding decision issued in October 1989 stated that while a landing requirement is a legitimate conservation measure, 100 percent of the catch need not be landed and counted. Canada agreed to abide by the panel's ruling, but the two countries disagreed over the report's policy implications. A binational panel was also established to review a Canadian complaint against U.S. restrictions pertaining to the size of imported live lobsters.

Chapter 19 of the FTA establishes two important thrusts for dealing with bilateral disputes in antidumping and countervailing duty cases. Current U.S. and Canadian trade remedy laws will continue to be unilaterally applied, thus allowing private interests to make their case for duties against imports "dumped" or "subsidized" by the other country. However, under the FTA either country will now be able to appeal the administration of these laws to a binational review panel instead of to a higher court in the country in question. The panels are to be composed primarily of international trade attorneys selected from lists compiled by each government. If decisions made by the domestic administering authority (in the United States, either the Department of Commerce or the International Trade Commission; in Canada, either the Department of National Revenue or the International Trade Tribunal) are challenged, the review panel will determine whether domestic laws were correctly and fairly applied. Either government can initiate the review process and will automatically respond to an individual request to do so, if the individual could otherwise have challenged the decision and initiated the judicial review process in court. The panel decision must be reached within 315 days after the request for a panel is made, thus expediting review, and will provide a timetable for remedial action. Final decisions by the binational panel will be binding on both governments.

As of the end of 1989, Canada had filed the majority of the requests for Chapter 19 panel review. Three cases involving the alleged dumping of red raspberries from British Columbia were nearing completion in early 1990. The panel found that the U.S. Department of Commerce calculation of dumping margins was adequate in one case but defective in the two other instances. Under the terms of Chapter 19, the determination was remanded to the Commerce Department "for action not inconsistent with the panel's decision," that is, for recalculation of the margins. Other cases pending under Chapter 19 panel review include the 1989 determinations by the Department of Commerce that Canadian pork producers were subsidized and by the International Trade Commission that material injury to U.S. producers resulted from Canadian pork imports. The accumulated decisions in Chapter 19 cases will provide important precedents to complement national judicial review.

Chapter 19 also provides for binational panel review of changes in either country's current antidumping or countervail laws to ensure consistency with the GATT and the FTA. If the panel recommends legislative modifications and if remedial action is not enacted within a specified period, the government requesting review can take equivalent action or terminate the agreement. This provision is an important gain for Canada since Canada must be specifically named as subject to any new changes in U.S. trade laws.[6] The two countries also agreed that the provisions of Chapter 19 will apply for a period of five to seven years, during which time negotiators will try to develop mutually advantageous rules governing subsidies and antidumping and countervailing duties. Furthermore, either government may terminate the FTA on six-months notice if no agreement on this issue is reached after seven years.

While the FTA and its dispute resolution mechanism do not guarantee Canadian access to the U.S. market (an objective which may be unrealistic between two sovereign nations), the binational panels and Canada–U.S. Trade Commission represent important innovations in institutional development. Specific procedures for notification and consultation, timetables, and legally binding decisions are significant improvements over current GATT mechanisms (Steger, 1988).

UNRESOLVED ISSUES IN CANADA–U.S. TRADE

The FTA made notable gains in liberalizing bilateral trade in goods and services and investment flows and in introducing new standards in several areas of multilateral trade negotiations. Nonetheless, agreement could not be reached in negotiations on several difficult issues. We discuss some of the more significant unresolved bilateral trade issues in this section.[7]

Subsidies

Perhaps the most important issue outstanding is the question of subsidies. Domestic subsidies are permissible under GATT rules, but countervailing duties may be applied if an importing country's industry is injured by goods receiving a subsidy in the exporting country. The critical issue is to determine what constitutes a countervailable subsidy. The definition of subsidy is complicated by the various forms it can take: grants, interest–free loans, loan guarantees, and tax credits or concessions, to name but a few.

Canadians have long charged that U.S. trade remedy law, while consistent with the GATT, may be administered in unpredictable and often politically biased ways (see Rugman's paper in this volume and Rugman and Anderson, 1987). From 1980 to mid-1987, Canada and the United States each initiated 44 trade remedy investigations of the other country. While Canada initiated twice as many antidumping cases as the United States, there was only one Canadian countervail investigation of U.S.

goods compared to eleven investigations of Canadian goods by the United States. Six of the U.S. investigations resulted in countervailing duties being assessed against about $4.2 billion (Cdn.) of Canadian exports over the period (Canada Department of Finance, 1988). Canadians argue that even if ultimately no countervailing duty is applied to Canadian exports, the expense of defending their interests and the uncertain outcome of the process can create substantial additional costs for firms wishing to conduct business in the United States.

The United States has a different perception of the subsidy problem, viewing it as a matter of controlling the pervasive use of Canadian subsidies which, directly or indirectly, enhance Canadian exports. The divergent perspectives—U.S. concern over the widespread use of subsidies and Canadian concern over the remedy of countervail—make bilateral negotiations on this issue difficult. Another complicating factor is that Canadian subsidies are perceived to have international ramifications, whereas U.S. subsidies are viewed as largely a domestic matter. Because of the greater relative importance of foreign trade in Canada, subsidies to Canadian firms are more likely to have a direct impact on bilateral trade. By contrast, U.S. subsidies may displace some imports by lowering production costs but are not often critical to export enhancement (Hart, 1989).

An example of the subsidy/countervail issue occurred in 1986 when the U.S. lumber industry alleged that Canadians unfairly subsidized exports of softwood lumber through low stumpage fees (payments for harvesting timber from government lands). Three billion dollars (Cdn.) of Canadian exports were at stake. The U.S. Department of Commerce investigation found that Canadian exports enjoyed a countervailable subsidy of 15 percent. However, a similar allegation three years earlier had resulted in a Commerce Department determination that Canadian stumpage fees were *not* countervailable. The different decisions seemed to rest on interpretation of the "specificity test": if a domestic practice is generally available and not specific in its benefits, then it is not considered to be countervailable. Canadians were irritated by the unilateral, narrower interpretation of this test by the United States in its later determination (Wonnacott, 1987).

Canadian negotiators had hoped that the FTA would identify allowable as well as countervailable subsidies, thereby removing a major bilateral trade irritant. Some progress was made in the automobile sector. In recent years, Canada has attracted Asian direct investment through duty-remission incentives based on export performance from Canada. The United States, the logical destination for such exports, argued that this policy amounted to an export subsidy to off-shore auto producers located in Canada. In the FTA, Canada agreed to eliminate this particular program. Agreement was also reached to eliminate export subsidies in bilateral agricultural trade, yet much less progress was achieved toward defining subsidies more generally. Because of unresolved issues involving the definition, visibility, and appropriate response to subsidies, both countries agreed to continue negotiations over a five to seven year period in an attempt to find a mutually acceptable definition of a trade-distorting subsidy and to impose more discipline on the use of subsidies and countervailing duties. However, both sides also indicated a desire to await the outcome of the current GATT multilateral negotiations before concluding an agreement bilaterally.

A factor complicating the ongoing subsidy negotiations is the differing visibility of subsidies in the two countries. Traditionally, Canadian government assistance has taken the form of industrial development grants, loan guarantees, regional development subsidies, and the like. While U.S. assistance also takes some of these forms, government assistance to the private sector, particularly at the federal level, is often less visible, appearing as tax credits, defense contracts, and low-interest loans.[8] At this time, there is little quantitative information on the extent of subsidies in the United States.[9] Thus, an important problem facing the negotiators is to come to agreement on the extent of subsidization in each country.

Other important trade policy disagreements face the negotiators. Canada is not alone among industrialized countries in making far less use of countervailing investigations than the United States. Indeed, U.S. trade remedy laws involving antidumping and countervail have become an important instrument of U.S. protectionism in the recent past (Hart, 1989). The Omnibus Trade and Competitiveness Act of 1988 continues this trend. This disproportionate use of countervail does not facilitate bargaining in the bilateral negotiations. Further, under Canada's Special Import Measures Act of 1984, consumer and user views of possible countervail determinations must be taken into account. These views are not considered in the U.S. investigation process, again complicating resolution of the subsidy issue in bilateral negotiations.

Investment

Important issues affecting bilateral investment also remain to be discussed. Canada has traditionally exhibited an ambivalence toward direct investment from the United States. While accepting virtually unlimited capital inflows for much of the period since World War II, investment restrictions undertaken by a review agency (Foreign Investment Review Agency) and discriminatory policies in the energy sector (National Energy Program) were institutionalized in the 1970s and early 1980s. In fact, such policies were an important issue for U.S. negotiators in the FTA deliberations. As discussed above, Canadian negotiators, for their part, were eager to obtain an exemption from the application of any future laws and regulations restricting foreign investment in the United States.

The FTA effectively commits the Canadian government to a less interventionist stance regarding U.S. direct investment in Canada, although significant restrictions remain on foreign investment in sensitive sectors, notably energy and culture. Furthermore, incentives designed to lure investment, practiced by all levels of government in both countries, remain undisciplined. The issue of internationally permissible incentives (which is tied to the subsidy negotiations) and extension of the FTA's coverage to additional sectors are likely topics for future negotiations.

Investment issues are also tied to the problem of adjustment, specifically to plant closures related to the more competitive trade environment. To the extent that U.S. investment in Canada's manufacturing sector has taken the form of branch plants shielded by high Canadian tariffs, firms will adjust to lower tariffs either by rationalizing production or closing plants. However, it is generally acknowledged that tariffs are not the primary reason for Canadian direct investment in the United States (see, for example, the papers by Rugman and Gandhi in this volume). Thus, the reduction and elimination of tariffs may not significantly influence bilateral direct investment, particularly if important nontariff barriers remain in place. Examples of such barriers are procurement policies of provincial, state, and local governments and federal departments currently not covered by the GATT procurement code, as well as federal government purchases of services.

Financial Services

Negotiations concerning financial services were complicated by several asymmetries, some of which were addressed in the FTA. In the United States, the Glass-Steagall Act prohibits banks from dealing in securities, while in Canada, financial deregulation has been proceeding at a much faster pace. U.S. banks operating in Canada are able to participate in more areas of business than in the United States. For example, domestic and foreign banks can own up to 100 percent of securities firms in Canada. In the United States, interstate operations of banks are restricted, whereas banks may operate an unlimited number of branches in Canada. While there are few federal obstacles to the establishment of Canadian financial institutions in the United States, foreign ownership and participation in the Canadian banking industry were prohibited until 1980.

Significant as the provisions of the FTA may be, the fact remains that deregulation may be more important than the trade agreement in liberalizing trade in financial services between Canada and the United States. Nevertheless, the FTA effectively insures a privileged place for each country's banks relative to other foreigners in the two national markets.

Adjustment Issues

Managing adjustment for workers and firms in import-competing industries promises to be an issue of political, if not economic, significance. In Canada, adjustment to the FTA occupies a higher profile because of the importance of international trade and foreign investment and the highly visible U.S. presence. Over 50 percent of the Canadian electorate voted in the 1988 federal election for a party opposed to the FTA and opposition interest groups have vowed to closely monitor the FTA's implementation. Adjustment issues are also important because each country's response to FTA-related dislocations (whether such dislocations are alleged or real) may be linked to the ongoing subsidy negotiations.

Trade liberalization, by definition, implies greater competition and the need for labor and capital to move from contracting industries to expanding ones. However, trade liberalization is only one of many factors forcing an economy to adapt. Technological developments, changing consumer tastes and preferences, and changes in factor prices also alter the structure of an economy. In the case of mature industries, governments are often under intense pressure to defend the interests of immobile resources such as workers in a particular region or the local property tax base. As a result, government intervention often takes the form of subsidies like those discussed earlier.

For this reason, bilateral agreement on the use of subsidies *without* agreement on the nature of adjustment policy may not be possible (Morici, 1989). Progress was made in the FTA to curb the use of many government practices which effectively distort trade by favoring domestic industry, such as some performance requirements on foreign investment, discriminatory energy-pricing, and duty-remission programs in the automobile sector. Nevertheless, other forms of intervention remain. Aggressive industrial policy to support high technology industries is one example that is readily apparent in both countries. The ongoing subsidy negotiations are one forum where an attempt may be made to further regulate the nature and extent of trade-distorting government intervention.

While workers and firms in import-competing industries will undoubtedly feel effects from greater competition, FTA-induced dislocations may be less significant than opponents of the agreement have predicted, for several reasons. First, the FTA incorporates a significant adjustment measure—namely the staged tariff reduction period—for industries likely to face more intense competition. Second, studies suggest that in Canada a high degree of mobility already exists in the manufacturing sector, and trade-sensitive industries are no exception. In a typical year, plant openings and expansions create slightly more jobs than are lost as firms contract or exit (Economic Council of Canada, 1988). Third, if the experience of other countries is any guide, much of the adjustment to freer trade will take the form of intraindustry and intrafirm rationalization, rather than shifts among sectors of the economy. Furthermore, in both countries the FTA will open markets for exports at the same time markets for imports are opened. Unlike import competition without the benefit of trade liberalization, more efficient sectors of each economy, particularly in Canada, should expand as less efficient ones contract. Appropriate macroeconomic policies and flexible exchange rates can also cushion the impact should adjustment become more difficult.

Implementation

Opposition interest groups in Canada have promised to closely monitor the FTA's implementation. Whether support continues for the FTA and the continuing negotiations depends, in part, on whether it is perceived to be providing the economic benefits its supporters had proclaimed. Assessing those benefits may be complicated by other economic events such as slower economic growth in the United States, changes in the Canada–U.S. exchange rate, or anti-inflationary monetary policy in Canada. As mentioned earlier, regulations having an impact on bilateral trade are being reviewed by binational panels established under Chapter 18 of the FTA. Numerous U.S. antidumping and countervail determinations also are being investigated and other trade disputes are being pursued through national channels or the GATT.

The FTA has not eliminated bilateral trade disputes during the first year of its implementation. It remains to be seen whether its rules and procedures will, on balance, lessen the nature and scope of irritants and improve the trading climate between the two nations. The success of phase two of the negotiations—talks dealing with subsidies, countervail, and antidumping, among other issues—will depend not only on progress in the Uruguay Round of GATT negotiations, but also on the perception that the FTA itself is a working improvement over previous conditions.

CONCLUSION

The papers presented in the following chapters discuss the challenges and opportunities likely to arise from the Canada–U.S. Free Trade Agreement, with attention to the global, national, and regional economies. Although the papers were originally presented at the October 1988 symposium held at Clarkson University, most have been updated to reflect a post–1988 election perspective. Business views emphasize adaptation and opportunity, while government and academic perspectives evaluate the implications of this innovative and historic agreement. The message is clear: Canada and the United States enjoy a remarkable opportunity to improve the competitiveness and efficiency of their respective economies. The two countries have also undertaken a significant challenge by creating innovative institutional procedures to resolve bilateral trade irritants and disputes. Many will be watching to see whether this latest form of bilateral cooperation will endure. We hope this book assists in understanding and assessing the implications of the Canada–U.S. Free Trade Agreement.

January 1990

TABLE 1

Foreign Trade: Canada and the United States

A. The Composition of Canada's Foreign Trade, 1988

Exports		*Imports*	
Exports of goods and services as a percentage of GDP	26.1	Imports of goods and services as a percentage of GDP	25.5

Main exports (percentage of merchandise exports)		Main imports (percentage of merchandise imports)	
Motor vehicles and parts	25.9	Producers' equipment	31.7
Other manufactured goods	19.9	Motor vehicles and parts	26.1
Nonferrous metals and minerals	13.5	Industrial materials	18.0
Pulp and paper	10.5	Consumer goods	10.7
Lumber and sawmill products	5.1		
Wheat	3.3		
Natural gas	2.2		

Main customers (percentage of merchandise exports)		Main suppliers (percentage of merchandise imports)	
United States	74.1	United States	69.1
Japan	6.0	Japan	6.2
United Kingdom	2.5	United Kingdom	3.6
Other EEC	5.3	Other EEC	8.3

TABLE 1 (cont.)

B. The Composition of United States' Foreign Trade, 1988

Exports		*Imports*	
Exports of goods and services as a percentage of GDP	11.2	Imports of goods and services as a percentage of GDP	12.7

Main exports (percentage of merchandise exports)		Main imports (percentage of merchandise imports)	
Machinery	27.4	Machinery	26.6
Transport equipment	14.5	Transport equipment	18.1
Chemicals	10.0	Manufactured goods	14.0
Food and live animals	8.2	Food and live animals	4.6
Crude materials (inedible)	7.8	Chemicals	4.5
Manufactured goods	7.1	Crude materials (inedible)	3.0

Main customers (percentage of merchandise exports)		Main suppliers (percentage of merchandise imports)	
EEC	23.3	Japan	20.1
Canada	23.0	EEC	19.0
Japan	11.8	Canada	18.9
Mexico	6.5	Taiwan	5.6

SOURCES: OECD, *Economic Surveys*, United States and Canada, 1988/89
Survey of Current Business, U.S. Department of Commerce

TABLE 2
U.S. Trade with Canada*
(billion U.S. dollars)

	Merchandise Exports	Percent of Total U.S. Exports	Merchandise Imports	Percent of Total U.S. Imports	Trade Balance	Services Exports	Services Imports	Bilateral Current Account Balance
1980	40.7	18.0	42.0	17.1	-1.3	15.2	6.6	7.3
1981	44.6	18.7	47.4	18.2	-2.8	15.1	5.8	6.5
1982	38.1	17.6	47.8	19.6	-9.7	14.6	5.1	-0.2
1983	43.1	21.0	54.8	21.2	-11.7	17.4	6.1	-0.4
1984	51.7	23.1	67.1	20.6	-15.4	18.6	7.3	-4.1
1985	53.9	24.6	69.6	20.2	-15.7	16.6	7.5	-6.6
1986	55.6	24.5	68.9	18.8	-13.3	18.1	7.0	-2.2
1987	61.1	25.2	73.8	18.2	-12.7	21.2	8.7	-0.2
1988	73.5	23.0	84.4	19.0	-10.9	25.5	11.2	3.4
1989	79.7	22.0	89.4	18.8	-9.7	25.3	11.8	3.8

*Data include adjustments for undocumented exports and other reconciliation adjustments. Imports are on a customs value basis.

SOURCES: Jeffrey J. Schott, U.S.-Canada Free Trade: An Evaluation of the Agreement, Institute for International Economics, Policy Analysis #24, April, 1988; U.S. Department of Commerce, Survey of Current Business, various issues.

TABLE 3
Leading Bilateral Merchandise Exports, 1988

A. Major United States Exports to Canada	Billion Canadian Dollars	Percent
Motor vehicle parts except engines	$13.3	14.7%
Passenger automobiles and chassis	8.6	9.5
Electronic computers	4.6	5.1
Trucks, truck tractors and chassis	2.7	3.0
Motor vehicle engines	2.1	2.3
Other telecommunications and related equipment	1.8	2.0
Electronic tubes and semiconductors	1.8	2.0
Aircraft complete with engines	1.4	1.6
Plastics materials, not shaped	1.2	1.3
Organic chemicals	1.1	1.2
All others	52.0	57.4
Total	90.6	100.0

B. Major Canadian Exports to the United States	Billion Canadian Dollars	Percent
Passenger automobiles and chassis	$16.8	17.2%
Motor vehicle parts except engines	7.7	7.9
Trucks, truck tractors and chassis	7.1	7.3
Newsprint paper	6.1	6.2
Crude petroleum	3.9	4.0
Softwood lumber	3.4	3.5
Wood pulp	3.0	3.1
Natural gas	2.9	3.0
Aluminum	2.5	2.6
Motor vehicle engines and parts	2.3	2.4
All others	42.1	43.0
Total	97.8	100.0

NOTE: Figures are reported for products on a customs basis; aggregate trade values shown elsewhere reflect adjustments for balance of payments purposes.

SOURCE: Statistics Canada, International Trade Division.

TABLE 4

U.S. Trade in Services with Canada, 1986-1988

(million U.S. dollars)

Category of Service	1986			1987			1988		
	Exports	Imports	Balance	Exports	Imports	Balance	Exports	Imports	Balance
Nonfactor Services									
Travel, fares, transportation	4,080	3,789	291	4,821	3,756	1,065	5,675	4,198	1,477
Fees, royalties	622	17	605	743	26	717	790	225	565
Other private services	1,956	524	1,432	2,181	755	1,426	3,181	1,650	1,531
Misc. government	32	97	-65	56	149	-93	33	114	-81
Total nonfactor services	6,690	4,427	2,263	7,801	4,686	3,115	9,679	6,187	3,492
Factor Services[1]									
Direct investment	5,180	53	5,127	7,022	896	6,126	8,954	1,082	7,872
Other private	6,171	1,934	4,237	6,292	2,148	4,144	6,882	2,615	4,267
U.S. government	48	600	-552	41	904	-863	31	1,300	-1,269
Total factor services	11,399	2,587	8,812	13,355	3,948	9,407	15,867	4,997	10,870

[1]Payments made by foreigners for the use of U.S. assets are classified as exports of the United States; payments made by U.S. citizens for the use of foreign assets are classified as imports of the United States.

SOURCE: U.S. Department of Commerce, *Survey of Current Business*, various issues.

TABLE 5
Stock of Bilateral Direct Investment, by Sector*

A. U.S. Foreign Direct Investment Position in Canada
   (book value at year-end, million U.S. dollars)

	1973	1980	1988
Manufacturing	11,755	18,802	28,859
Petroleum	5,320	10,573	11,679
Wholesale trade		3,899	3,516
Banking		N/A	778
Other finance, insurance and real estate	⎯► 8,467	6,136	10,868
Other		5,230	6,910
Total U.S. FDI in Canada	25,542	44,640	62,610

B. Canadian Foreign Direct Investment Position in the United States,
   (book value at year-end, million U.S. dollars)

	1973	1980	1988
Manufacturing	2,430	5,148	9,391
Merchandising	N/A	1,148	3,513
Mining	N/A	N/A	900
Petroleum	296	1,137	1,614
Banking and finance		354	2,058
Insurance	⎯► 320	444	2,993
Real estate		452	4,169
Other	998	1,036	2,724
Total Canadian FDI in United States	4,044	9,719	27,361

*See Note 1 to this introduction, p. 190.

SOURCE: U.S. Department of Commerce, *Survey of Current Business*, various issues.

TABLE 6

Leading Commodity Exports from Ontario and Quebec, 1988

	Million Canadian Dollars	Percent Destined for United States
A. Ontario:		
Passenger autos and chassis	$15,105	99%
Motor vehicle parts except engines	7,394	96
Motor vehicles for the transport of goods	6,327	99
Motor vehicle engines and parts	2,402	99
Precious metals	2,144	35
Office machines and equipment, including parts	1,878	81
Newsprint paper	1,546	100
Chemical wood pulp	876	94
Aircraft and spacecraft parts	745	91
Tractors	711	97
All other commodities	28,248	76
Total	67,376	86
B. Quebec:		
Newsprint paper	3,119	87
Aluminum, including alloys	2,675	82
Passenger autos and chassis	1,959	95
Other telecommunications and related equipment	1,097	87
Aircraft engines and parts	803	56
Wood pulp	640	56
Softwood lumber	525	84
Office machines and equipment	498	33
Copper, including alloys	496	81
Electricity	329	100
All other commodities	10,440	68
Total	22,581	75

SOURCES: Ontario, Ministry of Industry, Trade and Technology, Industry and Trade Research, 1990; Quebec, Bureau de la Statistique, Division du Commerce Exterieur, 1990.

TABLE 7
Selected Canadian-U.S. Commodity Trade Flows
and Tariff Levels, 1988, by FTA Staging Category

Commodity	Exports to U.S.	Imports from U.S.	Canadian Tariff (%)	U.S. Tariff (%)	Staging Category[1]
	(Million Canadian dollars)				
Vending machines	2.9	42.0	9.2-9.7	3.9	A
Fur apparel, other than mink	149.1	2.9	12.3-12.5	3.4-5.8	A
Ice skates	13.5	0.3	8.8-22.5	2.0-5.8	A
Whiskey	210.3	7.1	7.7	5.3-5.6	A
Computers and parts	1,646.3	4,753.7	3.9	3.7-3.9	A
Precious jewelry	1.1	1.1	13.3	6.5-7.0	B
Soap	20.3	17.4	12.8	3.1-7.7	B
Household furniture	291.3	148.6	15.0-15.3	2.5-6.6	B
Printed circuits[2]	311.4	362.9	10.3	5.3	B
Radar equipment and parts	35.5	59.2	9.5	4.9	B
Lawnmowers	38.4	77.6	10.2	4	C
Television receivers	67.4	154.4	8.2-9.5	3.9-5.0	C
Rail locomotives[2]	51.8	—	15	3.9	C
Self-propelled motor boats	40.3	110.0	15	1.5	C
Electronic tubes[2]	0.9	5.8	9.2	4.2	C

1 - A: tariffs eliminated on 1 January 1989
   B: tariffs phased out in five annual increments beginning 1 January 1989
   C: tariffs phased out in ten annual increments beginning 1 January 1989

2 - Tariffs for printed circuits, some electronic tubes, and diesel-electric rail
   locomotives were among those to be eliminated in 1990, according to the
   accelerated tariff reductions agreed to in November 1989.

SOURCE: Statistics Canada, *Exports, Merchandise Trade*, Catalogue 65-202;
        Imports Merchandise Trade, Catalogue 65-203, Ottawa, (1988)

TABLE 8
U.S. Dutiable Imports from Canada by
1985 Value and FTA Staging Category

SIC	Commodity	Dutiable Value (mil U.S. $)	Staging Class Distribution: (percent of dutiable value) Immediate	5-Year	10-Year	Average Duty (percent)
13	Crude petroleum and gas	4,429	0.0	100.0	0.0	0.3
35	Machinery	2,142	20.6	70.5	8.8	3.5
33	Primary metals	2,007	1.6	13.2	85.3	3.2
29	Refined petroleum	1,610	0.3	99.7	0.0	0.8
36	Electrical machinery	1,441	6.8	55.0	38.2	5.4
20	Food products	956	31.2	2.6	66.2	4.8
30	Rubber	863	0.0	0.0	100.0	4.4
34	Fabricated metals	792	0.3	16.0	83.7	4.5
28	Chemicals	790	3.1	82.7	14.3	8.7
37	Transportation equipment	724	2.6	14.6	82.8	3.3
38	Instruments	438	10.8	20.1	69.1	3.7
25	Furniture and fixtures	437	0.0	99.9	0.1	5.3
26	Paper	341	0.0	76.1	23.9	3.5
24	Wood products	266	0.2	69.2	30.6	4.9
32	Stone, clay, and glass	258	11.0	21.1	67.5	4.3
	Other	1,554	—	—	—	—
	Total all commodities	19,056	7.0	58.1	34.9	3.3

SOURCE: B.F. Shea, *The Canada-United States Free Trade Agreement: A Summary of Empirical Studies and An Industrial Profile of the Tariff Reductions.* Washington: U.S. Department of Labor, 1988, 21; Jeffrey J. Schott, *U.S.-Canada Free Trade: An Evaluation of the Agreement,* Institute for International Economics, Policy Analysis #24, April, 1988.

TABLE 9
Canadian Dutiable Imports from the United States by
1985 Value and FTA Staging Category

SIC	Commodity	Dutiable Value (mil U.S. $)	Staging Class Distribution: (percent of dutiable value)			Average Duty (percent)
			Immediate	5-Year	10-Year	
35	Machinery	2,838	38.6	52.6	8.8	7.4
36	Electrical machinery	1,661	0.2	34.9	64.9	10.4
28	Chemicals	1,283	0.3	71.1	28.6	10.8
34	Fabricated metals	1,013	0.2	22.0	77.8	10.3
37	Transportation equipment	943	6.0	8.7	85.3	10.2
38	Instruments	829	48.9	12.1	39.0	7.1
30	Rubber	741	0.1	16.6	83.3	13.1
33	Primary metals	724	18.1	5.7	76.2	6.9
20	Food products	701	2.8	11.7	85.5	8.8
26	Paper	513	0.0	87.0	13.0	8.8
	Other	2,294	–	–	–	13.3
	Total all commodities	13,540	13.0	33.6	53.4	9.9

SOURCE: B.F. Shea, *The Canada-United States Free Trade Agreement: A Summary of Empirical Studies and An Industrial Profile of the Tariff Reductions*. Washington: U.S. Department of Labor, 1988, 21; Jeffrey J. Schott, *U.S.-Canada Free Trade: An Evaluation of the Agreement*, Institute for International Economics, Policy Analysis #24, April, 1988.

PART I

OVERVIEW OF ECONOMIC OPPORTUNITIES:

Global Impact

1

JAMES R. TARRANT ⎯⎯⎯⎯⎯⎯⎯⎯⎯⎯⎯⎯⎯⎯⎯⎯⎯⎯

Overview and Highlights of the
Free Trade Agreement

My remarks are organized in four parts. I will, first, give the briefest of histories on how we got where we were in October 1988; second, highlight some key aspects of the Canada–U.S. Free Trade Agreement (FTA); third, look at the situation that existed in Canada during the federal election campaign in which the FTA played a major role; and, lastly, consider how the FTA fits with what the rest of the world has been doing.

Let me start with a bit of history. I think it is worth recalling that the current agreement is part of a long historical process. It did not just come out of thin air at the Shamrock Summit in 1985, and it does not represent any great leap of faith into the unknown. You can trace it back at least to 1854 when we had the first bilateral trade agreement. In 1911 and again in 1947 we also came very close to having a free trade agreement between the two countries. However, 1935 really represents a better starting point for the current bilateral agreement. That is when we began in the United States to dismantle the very high Smoot-Hawley tariffs which we had established during the Great Depression in the United States. So, for me, 1935 marks the beginning of a long path that we are still moving along today. The process is a long, gradual, incremental lowering of barriers between the two countries and the beginning of closer business relations and stronger economic ties between our two countries.

Of course, the Shamrock Summit marked the actual beginning of the negotiations, which took place over two long, difficult years. The negotiations ended at midnight on 3 October 1987 in Secretary of Treasury James Baker's office, when we all shook hands and cut the final deal. In a real sense, however, what we in government were doing throughout this whole process was catching up, providing a predictable framework to facilitate what business had already done and helping to expand the direction in which commerce would naturally flow anyway.

The Canada–U.S. Free Trade Agreement itself is, as I am sure you will appreciate, a very complicated agreement. In most versions it runs some 1200 pages and I will leave it to the experts and to your own research and reading to cover the specifics. But I would like to make just a few comments about the central thrust of the agreement and three or four of its most important elements.

The essential thrust of the FTA is to lower trade barriers, to liberalize trade wherever possible, to provide predictability, to instill the principle of national treatment wherever we can, and to build mechanisms to prevent backsliding when the political winds buffet the governments on both sides of the border. We do not hear much about the last point, but I think that is a very important underpinning of the agreement.

Let me look at just four of the many aspects of the FTA: tariffs, dispute settlement, energy, and subsidies. Obviously the phasing out of tariffs over the course of ten years is the heart of the agreement. Some were to go immediately in January 1989; some were to be phased out over five years and some were to be removed over ten years. Let me give you some examples of tariffs on certain key products as of October 1988. It is sometimes said that tariffs are not really an obstacle to trade, but in the case of U.S.–Canada trade, they have been an obstacle. If you were a clothing exporter to Canada, prior to the FTA there was about a 25 percent tariff; if you exported leather footwear, you paid about 20 percent; the duty on furniture averaged 13 percent, on toiletries, 10 percent—the list goes on. Tariffs have represented a hurdle, and tariff removal will mean increased sales for business. It also will mean lower prices and better selection for consumers. Competition is what it's all about, and this agreement is designed to bring greater competition to the marketplace.

Much has been said about Canada–U.S. trade disputes and how they should be settled. Dispute settlement is a major issue on the Canadian side of the border. Since 1980, Canada has launched approximately fifty trade complaints against the United States and the United States has launched about the same number going the other way. What the FTA does regarding dispute settlement is to set up a commission to establish binational panels of experts which provide mechanisms to consult informally and, if necessary, to have formal hearings and to reach binding decisions in some areas of disagreement. Americans and Canadians retain the basic right of redress that they have with their existing trade laws. Most significantly from the U.S. perspective, what we have done is to replace the final court challenge that was available with a binding dispute settlement mechanism.

Energy has been a very neuralgic issue in Canada. It is a very sensitive issue because of the feeling that sometimes natural resources are the only thing that United States wants from Canada. To insure that Canada would be a reliable supplier and that the United States would be a dependable purchaser, an energy chapter was included in the agreement. Its purpose was to provide protection for U.S. consumers in the event of a Canadian government, and I emphasize *government*, decision to reduce energy production and exports, for whatever purposes. The agreement provides predictability and certain types of guarantees. The key here, I think, is that the heavy hand of government is essentially removed from market forces and that there is protection in the event of government decisions. Let me underscore, lastly, with the regard to energy, that water was not discussed in the negotiations and is not part of the agreement. It is, however, governed by a number of other treaties between the two countries.

Finally, let me say that we were not successful in all areas. As much as we tried, we were unable to reach any sort of agreement on subsidies. Therefore, what we have done is set up a five to seven year period in which we will examine the question of subsidies in some detail. We could not get agreement in transportation, unfortunately, nor could we get agreement on beer. We were unable to reach agreement on a number of items, but I think we have in place an atmosphere, an environment, and a mechanism which will allow us to pursue some of these particulars in the future.

Next, let me take a minute to talk about the situation in Canada. I think sometimes we in the United States are not fully appreciative of what occurs on the other side of the border. It does not attract the attention of the U.S. media as much as American affairs do in Canada. A Canadian election was called for November 1988, precipitated by a decision on the part of the Liberal Party to withhold approval of the Free Trade Agreement in the Canadian Senate, which is not an elected body but rather an appointed group.

It is not an oversimplification to say that the FTA was the central issue of the campaign and that it precipitated an intensely emotional debate. It raised questions of great sensitivity for

Canadians: culture, national identity, environmental issues. In a sense, what we witnessed was that the agreement became a surrogate for a number of issues, most importantly the relationship that Canada wants to have with the United States.

I think it is important that we in the United States be alert and sensitive to these concerns. Most of the Canadian business community favored the deal, especially the energy, manufacturing, and financial sectors. Major opposition came largely from the cultural industries, nationalist groups, most unions, and the Premier of Ontario, David Peterson. My personal assessment was that anything short of a majority government on the part of the Conservatives would have meant that the agreement would not have been approved by the Canadian parliament.

Let me conclude with a few remarks on what the FTA means globally. A number of people have implied that we are building Fortress North America with this agreement. That is not the case. We have lowered barriers between the two countries, but we have retained exactly the same external tariff regulations and policies with regard to third countries. It is not an act of isolationism in any way. We have been very consistent with the long term policies and practices of the United States in attempting to liberalize world trade. What we are seeing these days is a great deal of globalization in trade, specifically in the energy, steel, insurance, and banking sectors, to name but a few.

The second major theme is that we are seeing regionalization at the same time. Principally, we have the Canada–U.S. Free Trade Agreement, but just a few years ago, a trade agreement between Israel and the United States was also concluded. There is also the Australia–New Zealand Agreement. As we look forward to 1992, the prospect of completion of the internal market in Europe must be watched very carefully.

The Canada–U.S. Free Trade Agreement is a powerful model. It is also a catalyst for what we would like to see done in the rest of the world in the way of trade liberalization. We think that the FTA will allow us to have some leverage and assure that we move ahead in the Uruguay Round of GATT negotiations. We hope that it will also represent a message to the European Community that we are looking forward to 1992 as being a liberalizing effort. Almost everything in the world today is moving toward economic openness, decentralization, deregulation, and privatization. The Canada–U.S. Free Trade Agreement is on the right side of both history and economics.

2

ALAN M. RUGMAN _____

Adjustments by Multinational Firms to Free Trade

My remarks focus on appropriate strategies for businesses—small business and bigger firms—now that we have entered into this era of "free trade" between the United States and Canada. I will begin by giving some introductory comments from a Canadian perspective about why Canada wanted to have a formal agreement with its largest trading partner. The first reason is size. Canada has a population of 25 million. This fact is significant when the world is moving towards protectionist trade blocks. Today the great bulk of international trade and investment is conducted in the Triad nations: the United States, Japan, and the European Community. Much of this trade is done by large multinational firms. In my career studies of multinationals, we have identified some 12,000 multinational enterprises in the world, the largest 500 of which conduct 80 percent of all foreign direct investment. Virtually all of these 500 firms are in the Triad nations; Canada has about 20 world class multinationals. These firms are the focal point of international activity.

There is tremendous competition between and amongst the multinationals from these nations. Furthermore, in the United States—the engine of postwar economic prosperity— there has been a definite emergence of protectionism in recent years. This has been a great threat to Canada, the largest trading partner of the United States. Thus, the primary reason Canadian businesses wanted a free trade agreement with the United States was to obtain secure access to the huge U.S. market.

Canadians have debated how their trade patterns could be diversified. We would like to have more trade with Japan. Indeed, our trade with Japan has doubled in the last ten years, going from 3 percent of our exports to 6 percent. We also have about 8 percent or 9 percent of our trade with the European Community. But more than three-fourths of our trade is with the United States, so it is imperative to have a secure set of rules in order to make long term investment decisions.

A new form of protectionism has emerged in the United States. Most U.S. citizens, quite correctly, do not regard the application of trade remedy laws as protectionism. These laws allow countervailing duties and antidumping duties to be imposed if foreigners are subsidizing their exports or selling them below cost. The sanctions imposed are consistent with the rules of the General Agreement on Tariffs and Trade (GATT), of which both Canada and the United States are members. The GATT Subsidies Code in the Tokyo Round allows countries like Canada and the United States to take measures against foreigners who are subsidizing certain industries.

Policies which we in Canada regard as internal transfer payments—unemployment insurance, which is universally available across the country; Medicare, another universally available program; and programs for regional development which are enshrined in our Constitution—are often viewed by outsiders as indirect subsidies to our exporting firms. These policies can sometimes get caught up in the quasi-judicial process of applying trade remedy laws.

In my opinion, perfectly legal antidumping statutes are subject to a bias in their administration. The International Trade Commission and the U.S. Department of Commerce, from the perspective of Canadians affected by their actions, may have been bowing to political pressures. My book, *Administered Protection in America*, analyzed fifty cases involving Canada: the Fresh Atlantic Groundfish Case, the Softwood Lumber Case, and recent cases involving potash, steel, hogs, and so on. After reading these reports, I concluded that there was an insufficient amount of objective analysis being done, perhaps due to time constraints, but also partly because of political pressures on these agencies.

Even well-trained colleagues of mine in the economics profession can make fundamental mistakes in their view of the world. When a businessperson from the United States quite appropriately uses trade remedy measures to initiate an investigation and cites the unemployment insurance payments to East Coast Atlantic fishermen as a subsidy, Canadians become quite upset. The primary purpose of unemployment insurance payments to these fishermen is *not* to give an export subsidy to a Canadian firm. It is to help relieve the poverty in Newfoundland, Cape Breton, and other poor areas of Canada.

As another example, the Bethlehem Steel Company launched a countervail and antidumping action on steel rails, citing electricity in Canada as being a form of subsidy because of the state's involvement in the energy sector. Again, it is galling to think that the legal process will result, I predict, in a ruling by the International Trade Commission that the U.S. firm sustained material injury. Unemployment insurance and low-cost electricity are generally available in Canada. But if you look at it from the perspective of the United States, certainly the fish are exported and the low-cost electricity results in additional exports of steel. So it is easy to make a mistake in the analysis: was the issue a targeted subsidy or was it something essential to the Canadian way of life?

The trouble—and I would like to stress this as a major point—is that we Canadians live in a small open economy where nearly 30 percent of GDP is traded. Canada is a thin country spread over 4,000 miles. We need to have a strong role for government; we need to have unemployment insurance, Medicare, and what may appear to be subsidies but what are, in fact, not really subsidies at all.

Building on this fear of U.S. trade law actions, the business community in Canada lobbied the government very strongly and, as a result, an agreement was negotiated. The government established an International Trade Advisory Committee and fifteen sectoral advisory groups on international trade. We got a deal which was generally acceptable to the business community, both small and large business, though in Canada there are, of course, some concerns about how to adjust to free trade.

The bulk of my research suggests that there really is not an adjustment issue for the large multinationals because these firms are already highly integrated. Essentially, U.S.–Canadian trade and investment is conducted by fifty multinational firms. Seventy percent of all U.S.–Canadian trade and investment is done by about twenty-five U.S. subsidiaries in Canada and about twenty-five Canadian-owned firms. These are large firms with over one billion dollars of sales. But large firms are not alone in supporting the FTA; small businesses in Canada also support the agreement because they see more opportunities for getting into the U.S. market.

A simple summary of management theory provides a framework for analyzing adjustment in which we can distinguish between country-specific factors which capture the resource strength of Canada and which may be influenced by tariff and nontariff barriers to trade. In the competitive advantage matrix shown in Figure 1, the vertical axis represents country-specific advantages (CSAs) which increase as we move up the axis. The horizontal axis represents firm-specific advantages (FSAs) which are proprietary to corporations. Examples of FSAs include a technology-based research and development advantage, but there can also be advantages in marketing.

Most multinational firms are located in quadrant one. These firms are already successful and can pursue any of three management strategies, as defined by Michael Porter (1980). The first is a cost-leadership strategy based on scale economies, with competition on the basis of price. This strategy is represented in quadrant one. Secondly, firms can have a product differentiation strategy represented by brand-name products. Quadrant two is the matrix location for this strategy. Firms in this quadrant generally exhibit strong firm-specific advantages in marketing and customization. These advantages dominate, so in serving demand-driven markets, the country-specific advantages are not essential. Thirdly, it is possible to have a focus strategy, which builds upon cost considerations. Quadrant three firms are generally in mature globally-oriented industries, producing largely a generic product. Given their late stage in the product life cycle, production FSAs from the possession of intangible skills are less important that the CSAs of location and energy costs. Thus these firms generally follow low-cost strategies. Quadrant four firms represent inefficient, foundering firms with no consistent strategy nor any intrinsic CSAs or FSAs. These firms are therefore preparing to either restructure or exit.

With free trade, changes in CSAs may result in changes to the entry and exit barriers associated with a particular industry or product line. Following Porter, these entry barriers can be grouped as: economies of scale, capital requirements, switching costs, access to distribution channels, cost disadvantages independent of scale, and government policy. By affecting competition, these changes determine whether a switch in matrix positioning or competitive strategy will be necessitated by free trade.

Free trade will affect the strategic planning of firms differently depending on their initial positioning in the matrix. A firm in quadrant one faced with declining CSAs will probably not have to change its cost leadership strategy. If the decline is substantial, the firm may move to the second quadrant where it will place greater emphasis on niching and following a focus/differentiation strategy. A quadrant three firm, which by definition has weaker FSAs and thereby follows a focus low-cost strategy, will move to quadrant four and face restructuring or exit. A firm in the second quadrant with strong FSAs initially will sustain its strategy unless the original CSA had been internalized into a FSA. In such cases, the weakened FSA will necessitate a move to quadrant four and either exit or restructure. The converse of these cases is given by the scenario of an increase in the strengths of the CSAs. In this case the quadrant four firm can internalize these new CSAs and move to the first quadrant.

In terms of business strategy, quadrants one and four have unambiguous implications. A firm in the first quadrant can benefit from a low-cost or niching strategy. Such firms are constantly evaluating their product mix. As a firm's product line matures, then declines, the firm eventually graduates to quadrant four. By adopting new product lines and maintaining an effective strategy, the firm can maintain its overall positioning. Similarly, in the fourth quadrant there is no alternative to restructuring or exit.

Quadrants two and three can be credible positions for different types of firms. For instance, a firm in the second quadrant which benefits from strong FSAs in marketing or vertical integration can offset a weak CSA. Such firms are only threatened to the degree that a foreign competitor also builds on a strong CSA. However, this is not the case for multinational firms in the second quadrant as their position seems to be industry-specific. In contrast, mature multinational enterprises (MNEs) in quadrant three can build on internal FSAs, making it possible for them to move to the first quadrant.

Although the first three quadrants represent appropriate positioning for some firms, there exists an asymmetry between the second and third quadrants. A quadrant two strategic choice may be stable for some firms; however, quadrant three firms should aim for quadrant one. This asymmetry is rooted in the fact that CSAs (as modeled here) are exogenous to the firm while FSAs are not. To the extent that CSAs can be influenced by government protection, there is always increased uncertainty associated with such strategies. For an efficient quadrant two firm, there is no need and little incentive to move to the first quadrant. If the firm has a conglomerate structure, it would be more useful to situate each product line individually as they may have different strategies. On the other hand, small businesses will generally follow niching strategies.

Large multinationals today often need to combine scale economies with marketing skills. In terms of the competitive advantage matrix, my analysis suggests that most of the Canadian MNEs and U.S. subsidiaries are in quadrant one. Table 10 presents a list of the Canadian-owned multinationals which have been successful in international business. These megafirms are ranked by size; all had 1986 sales in excess of $1 billion (Cdn.) and derive at least 25 percent of their sales from foreign markets. These firms are already very active internationally. The five-year average ratio of foreign to total sales is 67 percent, and 42 percent of their assets are located outside Canada (see Rugman, 1988a). These firms include Alcan, in aluminum; Northern Telecom, in digital telephone-switching equipment; and some twenty other firms. Most of these firms are resource-based; most are operating in quadrant one; and most will remain there after free trade. To some extent, the mineral-based firms might be placed in quadrant three because of their financial performance in recent years. The recession of the early 1980s drove down their return on equity, pushing these firms more into quadrant three than quadrant one.

To understand the strategic decisions made by these firms in adjusting to this new trading environment, we will analyze them in their industry groups and position them in Figure 1. These twenty-two megafirms can be divided according to their principal operations into minerals, pulp and paper, distilleries, high technology, oil and gas, and manufacturing.

The firms in the minerals sector were hit hard by the 1981–82 recession and the decline in world mineral prices. As a result, they have tended to emphasize low-cost strategies. In addition, they have tried to move up the value-added chain in processing and manufacturing. These mature resource-based firms are situated in the third quadrant, except for Alcan in quadrant one. The principal reason for this positioning has been their financial performance.

As with the minerals megafirms, the pulp and paper firms benefit from CSAs because of their access to Canadian forests. They have managed to internalize long term contracts in these forests into FSAs of a vertically integrated production structure. The firms in this sector will benefit greatly from the dispute settlement procedures of the FTA (see Rugman, 1988b). These procedures should insulate these firms from the abusive application of U.S. trade law procedures by rival firms seeking a competitive edge.

All of the liquor and beer firms follow focus differentiation strategies and are situated in the second quadrant and, as they operate in a mature industry, each is diversifying. Labatts derives greater revenue from its agri-food divisions and has been integrating across the U.S. border. Molson has diversified into chemicals and retail merchandising and these divisions now account for over one-half of the firm's profits. Seagram's has also diversified into upscale premium products. Its strategic equity link (22 percent ownership) to DuPont Chemicals has provided the source of capital for this diversification.

Two nontraditional Canadian megafirms are represented by the high-technology innovators, Northern Telecom and Moore. The FSAs that these firms rely on are research and development, marketing, and service adaptability. The CSAs upon which they have built include proximity to the U.S. market and some domestic protection. Nortel is a quadrant one firm benefiting from its link to Bell and its research unit, Bell Northern. Moore is a firm in the second quadrant, following a focus/niching strategy. Its emphasis on customization has made its FSAs dominate its CSAs. Both of these firms are well diversified along geographic and product lines. Thus, bilateral trade liberalization would only enhance their competitive strengths.

The manufacturing sector consists of five firms in mature industries: Ivaco, AMCA, Varity, Magna International, and Bombardier. The FSAs possessed by these firms include an integrated structure, marketing skills associated with brand names, and a reputation for quality. For the most part, cost and price concerns have dominated the strategies of these firms. However, some, like Ivaco in steel products and Magna in automotive parts, have managed to move up a value-added chain to service products and geographic market niches.

AMCA and Varity are undergoing major restructuring of their operations, dropping core product lines and seeking new ones, such as auto parts and engines for Varity. Bombardier and Magna have been successful firms in quadrant two emphasizing focus differentiation strategies and customization. Ivaco, a world leader in several steel and wire products, is situated in the first quadrant. Trade liberalization should not adversely affect these three firms.

To summarize, trade liberalization should enhance the strategic positioning of most of these Canadian megafirms. In adjusting to the new competitive global economy, these firms have rationalized their operations to obtain appropriate configuration and coordination advantages.

We can apply the same framework to the U.S. subsidiaries in Canada. Again, studies reveal that successful firms will continue to service the Canadian market from Canadian locations after free trade. The major problems will be with firms in food processing or with firms that are in Canada simply to avoid tariffs. Those branch plants whose presence is due to unnatural market imperfections, such as tariffs, will face low exit barriers and will move to the fourth quadrant. However, those whose presence is attributed to other unnatural market imperfections, and who have therefore developed compensating FSAs, may remain. If the parent firm possesses FSAs that can be transferred to the subsidiary, it may be reorganized to remain in Canada.

The firms listed as U.S. subsidiaries in Canada, shown in Table 11, are not all in Canada simply to avoid Canadian tariffs. Some may have located in Canada for access to natural resources, to benefit from marketing skills, or in other ways to service the Canadian market. With trade liberalization, the importers and local service firms will remain intact, as will the globally rationalized firms and those possessing world product mandates. These firms have different levels of managerial autonomy; however, they have an economic rationale beyond tariffs. The branch plants and satellite operations will more than likely either have to become globally rationalized or obtain world product mandates (see Crookell, 1987). Alternatively, their operations can be scaled down to import or to provide local service or, in the extreme, to exit. Clearly the process of moving towards global rationalization or obtaining a world product mandate will not be easy (see Rugman and Douglas, 1986; D'Cruz and Fleck, 1987). World product mandates will have to be earned by the subsidiary; they will not be routinely granted by the parent. Only when Canada possesses strong CSAs, or the subsidiary possesses potential FSAs of its own, will a shift in matrix positioning occur.

These classifications can be integrated into the competitive advantage matrix to interpret the effects of trade liberalization. In the first quadrant, the globally rationalized firms and world product mandates are building on strong CSAs and FSAs. In quadrant two, the importers and local service firms build on FSAs in marketing which dominate any potential CSAs. The inefficient tariff factories, the satellites, and branch plants are located in the third quadrant. With trade liberalization, these firms face the choice of restructuring or exit and may move to quadrant four. Again, they need to develop competitive strategies to move into the first or second quadrant.

The key megafirms listed in Table 11 can be situated into the quadrants of the competitive advantage matrix. What is striking is that most of these firms are situated in quadrant one. In fact, many of these firms have already begun to diversify to meet the new competitive global trading regime. For example, DuPont Canada has publicized its specialization to improve productivity and to obtain economies of scale (see Newall, 1988). Interestingly, with these increases in scale, companies have found that their production flexibility to produce smaller runs has helped them to compete in the United States, even against their parent company.

The first quadrant firms are led by the "Big Three" automobile producers: General Motors, Ford, and Chrysler. These firms benefit from the 1965 Canada–U.S. Auto Pact which established a managed trade arrangement for autos and auto parts. Other quadrant one firms building on CSAs particular to Canada and FSAs in marketing and production are the oil and gas companies: Imperial Oil, Texaco, Mobil Oil, Amoco, and Suncor. IBM Canada is also in the first quadrant. Its parent company has chosen a pattern of international operation that emphasizes local marketing and global rationalization of production.

This set of U.S. subsidiaries also contains firms positioned in the third quadrant. Canadian General Electric (CGE) has already begun to gear up to compete globally by producing inputs for MNEs in Canada doing business abroad. In addition, CGE has allied itself to global markets by acting as a part of a network of the globally rationalized General Electric system. This process has necessitated rationalization of some operations to specialize in certain product lines. With these changes, CGE should move from the third quadrant into the first. Dow Chemical Canada is located in quadrant three based on its financial performance over the last five and ten years. As indicated above, this performance is evidence of weak managerial FSAs. To move to the first quadrant, the firm has to solve these problems.

Procter and Gamble is a second quadrant firm. The CSAs upon which it builds are access to pulp and paper companies to reduce packaging costs as well as other products which are vital inputs into its production process. The firm builds on its parent's strong FSAs in marketing and established name brands; however, with trade liberalization its Canadian oriented subsidiary will have to adapt. Tariff protection forces an inefficient production scale on its operations and, in the new environment, this represents a weak FSA. As tariffs are reduced, intrafirm trade should increase and some rationalization should occur across the border. Procter and Gamble has estimated that brands accounting for 45 percent of its volume can be manufactured in Canada at a cost less than or equal to that in the United States (see Gove, 1988). Some other firms, such as Quaker Oats Limited, with food-processing operations, will suffer from the policies of agricultural marketing boards which raise input prices. These firms will have to restructure to become globally competitive or will end up moving to the fourth quadrant.

To summarize, the adjustment process of U.S. subsidiaries is dependent on the nature of their present autonomy and degree of internationalization. Perhaps more critical to successful adjustment is their potential to increase each of these variables. Studies for the Economic Council of Canada by Don McFeteridge found that foreign-owned subsidiaries adjusted their operations in response to past trade liberalization in the same manner as Canadian firms (Economic Council of Canada, 1988). A key conclusion of these studies is that trade liberalization has been associated with the retention rather than the flight of U.S.-owned firms.

Therefore, the conclusion of my work, based on surveys, questionnaires, and interviews with these firms, is that free trade will not present a major adjustment problem because big business is already highly integrated. What the agreement does is to recognize that integration; it will not suddenly cause more integration.

An April 1987 survey of CEOs of key Canadian multinationals and U.S. subsidiaries, as well as a follow-up survey in the spring of 1988, support this conclusion. The single most important finding of these surveys is that trade liberalization is welcomed by these firms. It was determined that: (1) multinationals can bear the costs of adjustment themselves; (2) there will be few plant closings; (3) bilateral trade and investment will increase; and (4) these large firms will continue to prosper. Seventy-five percent of these megafirms indicated that a Canada–U.S. trade agreement would be beneficial to them. The basis of support for free trade is rooted in the prevailing belief that the status quo is one of increasing protection. Sixty-three percent indicated that the status quo did not benefit them. On the question of adjustment to a bilateral trade agreement, 31 percent expected to face adjustment costs. However, 80 percent of the Canadian firms and 94 percent of the U.S. firms indicate that adjustment assistance would not be required.

My final point is that small business firms also will undoubtedly benefit from the agreement. While the bigger multinational firms could invest in staff and offices in each others' countries to reduce information costs, small business should now benefit from knowing the rules of the game. An analysis of how U.S. firms will react remains to be done by American scholars, but from the viewpoint of Canadian small businesses, they now have the opportunity to enter different regions of the United States, to find more and more market niches, and to do well. Their disadvantage is that American small businesses know the local market. Canadians will have to make some investment in becoming familiar with customers and providing them with high quality products and services. But there is a big incentive for Canadians to do that. In general, I would hypothesize that there is less incentive for American firms to rush up to Canada because the market is only one-tenth the size of the U.S. market. Most American small businesses, I believe, spread out into different regions of the United States. But ultimately, I think that small businesses, especially in areas like northern New York, would look to Canada as a region for business opportunities.

Let me conclude by drawing this together. From a Canadian perspective, business is hungry for free trade. Big business is already into the adjustment process and its strategic thinking has incorporated this fact. Eighty-five percent of small businesses in Canada support the Canada–U.S. Free Trade Agreement. I leave you with one final question. If this is such good news for Canada, why did we fight an election on it? My hypothesis is that it was because of misinformation and misunderstanding of the economic benefits and because of an unfounded fear of loss of sovereignty. However, in the sovereignty area, Canada has been very successful in the agreement. The cultural industries, the health sector, social services, and transportation were all exempted from the agreement. Canada stands to gain significantly from this agreement. While it is not perfect, it nevertheless provides substantial benefits and begins to resolve problems which impede efficiency and growth in both countries.

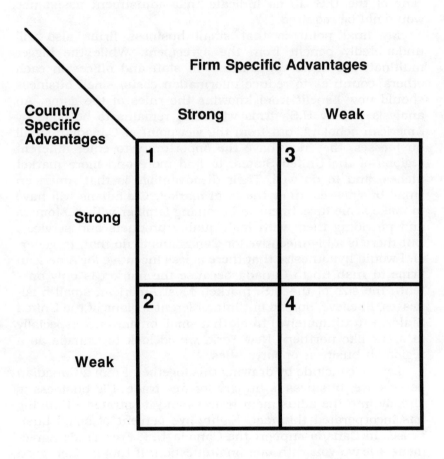

TABLE 10
Performance of the Largest Canadian Industrial Multinationals

Firm	1986 Sales (mil Cdn. $)	Return on Equity (ROE)[1]	
		1977-86	1982-86
Alcan	8222	3.4	10.7
Northern Telecom	6091	18.2	15.7
Seagram	4618	11.7	11.4
John Labatt	4253	18.4	16.9
Noranda	3547	0.1	8.8
Moore	2919	15.4	16.5
Abitibi-Price	2764	9.6	14.3
Nova	2681	10.2	10.9
MacMillan-Bloedel	2512	4.9	8.9
Domtar	2327	10.3	12.5
Molson	2250	12.7	15.1
Consolidated-Bathurst	2018	10.0	15.1
Ivaco	1945	5.1	12.1
Varity	1877	0.7	0.7
AMCA International	1498	2.9	10.9
Inco	1452	1.1	4.0
Gulf Canada[2]	1407	12.1	14.5
Cominco	1328	0.5	9.4
Falconbridge	1146	2.1	5.1
Bombardier	1104	8.8	7.0
Canfor	1047	2.2	n/a
Magna International	1028	18.2	20.5
Overall Average[2]	2574	8.0	11.3

NOTES: 1. ROE is calculated as net income before extraordinary items divided by average equity.
2. Gulf has been excluded from the totals and averages due to a change of ownership in 1985.

SOURCES: Corporate Annual Reports, *Financial Post* 500 (various issues)
IMF *International Statistical Yearbook* year-end exchange rate

TABLE 11
The Largest Canadian Subsidiaries of U.S. Multinationals

| Subsidiary | Return on Equity | | Matrix Position |
	5 yr. Average 1982-1986	10 yr. Average 1977-1986	Cell Number
G.M. of Canada	33.5	26.5	1
Ford of Canada	16.1	9.0	1
Chrysler Canada	130.9	65.8	1
Imperial Oil	9.5	13.2	1
IBM Canada[1]	28.8	25.5	1
Texaco Canada	17.4	19.3	1
Mobil Oil Canada	16.7	20.6	1
Canadian General Electric	9.5	10.3	3
Dow Chemical Canada[2]	2.1	10.0	3
Amoco Canada	18.7	18.9	1
Du Pont Canada	10.8	12.8	1
Suncor Canada	5.9	17.9	1
Procter & Gamble	15.1	17.9	2
Mean	15.3	14.5	

NOTES: Ranked by 1986 sales.
Negative ROEs have been set to zero.
Chrysler has been excluded from the means.
1. 4 and 9 year averages, respectively.
2. 3 and 8 year averages, respectively.

SOURCE: *Financial Post 500*, various years.

3

JEFFREY J. SCHOTT _____

The Implications of Freer Trade in Services

Trade in services is an important component of the bilateral economic relationship. Two-way trade in services between Canada and the United States was about $37 billion (U.S.) in 1988, including investment income and nonfactor services, and the United States had a bilateral surplus in that trade of more than $14 billion. In fact, the surplus in services trade more than offset the U.S. bilateral merchandise trade deficit with Canada of $10.9 billion. So, it is no wonder that almost 25 percent of the text of the Canada–U.S. Free Trade Agreement (FTA) is devoted to provisions on services, financial services, investment, and "temporary entry for business persons." My purpose is to provide some brief general comments on what the FTA says regarding services and some of the broader economic implications of the steps taken in the FTA both for bilateral trade and for the international trading system.

The agreement broke new ground by establishing firm contractual obligations on services for both countries. Before the FTA, services were really virgin territory for the international trading system. Bilateral service transactions had been substantially immune to international discipline for three reasons: first, the lack of coverage of services in the General Agreement on Tariffs and Trade (GATT); second, the absence of a bilateral treaty of friendship, commerce, and navigation between our two countries, which often contains provisions on services; and, third, the extensive reservations to the Organization for Economic Cooperation and Development (OECD) codes on invisibles and capital movements.

Now, how important is this? Some people have argued that we have not done so badly without strong trading rules. But trade in services is increasing substantially, especially if one also considers those services that are embodied in traded goods. Thus, barriers to trade in services can distort trade in both goods and services. That is why a lack of rules in this area is important and was a primary consideration of the negotiators of this agreement.

There is often reference to the problem of a level playing field in international trade. In services, the promotion of fair trade has been even more problematic because of the absence of international guidelines. The FTA goes a long way toward remedying that problem. Indeed, the FTA promotes fair trade in services by *creating* a playing field and *creating* rules for the game so that trade in services can be free and fair. The rules are elaborated in a framework of rights and obligations regarding the regulation of service industries. The FTA provisions do not necessarily seek to promote identical policies or regulations, but ones that are compatible with the agreed guidelines or principles set out in the FTA. And, importantly, the FTA commitments also apply to the policies of state and provincial governments, except in the area of financial services.

This said, the FTA is much better on rulemaking than on liberalization. Indeed, almost all existing restrictions on trade in services between our two countries have been grandfathered, which means they have been left intact. However, this is not a great problem in the bilateral context, given the relative openness of services trade compared to other markets and the low number of bilateral disputes that have arisen in the past.

Perhaps more importantly, the FTA contains a standstill obligation under which each country commits to refrain from new laws and regulations that discriminate against services provided by the other country. The purpose of this standstill is preemptive, to forestall future attempts to impose protection. The standstill does not require changes in existing policies, laws, or regulations, even if they have discriminatory effects, nor does the standstill obligation prevent either government from implementing changes in domestic policies and regulations. It does require, however, that any change not mask protectionist intent, nor discriminate against goods and services provided by U.S. and Canadian interests in either country. It basically sets an inventory date after which there will be no new restrictions, and any changes will move in the direction of liberalization rather than greater discrimination. The bottom line on the rulemaking is this: the greater certainty of the rules of the game and the scope of regulatory policies should help businesses to take better advantage of new trading opportunities. I think this is a very important point and a key aspect of the services provisions in the agreement.

Chapters 14 and 15 of the FTA set out the main rules and obligations for services other than financial services, which are covered separately in Chapter 17. The agreement applies to a broad range of service activities, but notably excludes transportation, cultural industries, and a range of government and social services.

FTA obligations in services cover five key areas. The first obligation involves national treatment, to prohibit new discrimination against foreign service providers in specified sectors. The second obligation involves the right of establishment or the right of commercial presence, to provide appropriate market access guarantees to insure that the national treatment obligation is meaningful. The national treatment obligation—to treat foreign firms the same as domestic firms—is only valuable if a foreign firm has effective commercial access to the domestic market. It does not help if a firm is accorded national treatment but cannot get into the market to begin with. Depending on the service, market access may involve the need to establish a presence in the market, the need to have access to distribution channels, the need to have equal access to operating licenses for activities in regulated industries, or the capability to relocate specialized management or technical personnel. FTA provisions ensure that transactions can be conducted across borders with access to the necessary marketing and distribution channels, thereby facilitating greater trade in services.

The third obligation involves licensing and certification procedures to ensure that, with limited exceptions, government regulators judge providers of services solely on their competence and not on their nationality. The fourth obligation involves procedures facilitating cross-border travel by business persons, an important issue in the border regions. One should note, however, that the FTA coverage of labor services is incomplete. Indeed, FTA provisions on labor services apply only to professional and technical services, investors and intracompany transferees, and not to the broader category of all labor services. This may reflect the fact that the key bilateral issue in the area of labor services involves the temporary entry of business persons. It also undoubtedly reflects the greater political sensitivity in both countries to temporary immigration of blue-collar workers.

The fifth obligation involves specific sectoral annexes. The three that are appended to the services chapter cover architecture, tourism, and computer and telecommunication network-based enhanced services. These sectoral annexes address specific restrictions and regulatory issues in each area. In addition, the FTA provides for the negotiation of other sectoral annexes to deal with the prospective rollback of existing restrictions that have been grandfathered under the FTA provisions. The basic point here is that while most of the FTA rules establish a standstill on service trade barriers, the sectoral annexes make it possible to liberalize existing restrictions.

Chapter 17 of the FTA contains the basic provisions on financial services, specifically commercial banking, investment banking, and trust and loan companies. Insurance is primarily covered by the services and investment chapters. The FTA provisions reflect both the substantial integration of the U.S. and Canadian markets that already exists and the trend toward deregulation in both countries in recent years. Indeed, in most respects the financial services provisions in this agreement continue the deregulatory course in financial markets that both governments have been pursuing. In the FTA, both governments have committed to liberalizing their markets, extending the resulting benefits to the firms of the other country, and establishing a consultative mechanism to oversee the liberalization.

As a result, we are likely to see two specific results. First, we will see continuing growth in the integration of North American financial markets. This does not mean that U.S. firms will dominate. Indeed, the size and the power of the major Canadian financial institutions make that very unlikely. But the FTA does provide new opportunities for U.S. firms to explore specific niches in the Canadian market, and these niches could be very profitable. Second, and perhaps even more important, the FTA will add fuel to the fire for financial market reform in the United States. We already are seeing efforts in Congress to reform the Glass-Steagall Act, efforts that will get even more attention as a result of changes in the marketplace brought about, in part, by the FTA. I suspect that was a key rationale of those U.S. firms that pushed hard for an agreement with Canada. One can look at American Express and others and see that their interests lay as much in enhancing deregulation in the U.S. market as in new openings in the Canadian market.

Let me conclude with a brief comment on some of the international implications of the agreement. The FTA provides a model of the type of umbrella code or framework agreement on services that the United States has been advocating in Geneva for several years. I should note that extension of the GATT discipline to services will be a key test of the success of the current Uruguay Round of trade negotiations in the GATT. FTA provisions regarding national treatment, establishment, and licensing and certification procedures are carefully crafted and could serve as a model for a GATT code. In fact, I think one of the important results of the Canada–U.S. Free Trade Agreement has been the education it has provided for both U.S. and Canadian negotiators. For the first time, U.S. and Canadian negotiators had to sit down and look at the problems of actually writing out contractual obligations in the area of services. They found that some of these obligations were much harder to craft than they had originally envisioned. The work that was involved over nearly two years of negotiations will be an important benefit to those negotiators in the GATT who are beginning to undertake a similar exercise.

I should emphasize, however, that the U.S.–Canadian pact can only be a useful first step toward a GATT accord. A successful GATT negotiation will require much more tangible results in the form of liberalization of specific trade barriers than was achieved in the agreement with Canada. In the U.S.–Canada context, barriers were not a substantial obstacle to trade and it was as important, if not more important, to establish a standstill provision on rulemaking so that one would have greater certainty in the conduct of future trade. But in the international negotiations there is going to be much greater emphasis on how existing trade barriers will be reduced.

The U.S.–Canada provisions will provide a model for the development of GATT rules, but that will be only one aspect of the GATT negotiations. However, the comprehensive standstill on new services trade barriers, relatively easily arrived at by the United States and Canada given the level of development and openness of their service sectors, will be a much more difficult objective to reach in the GATT. The principles contained in the services code may not be universally applied and countries may not want to subject certain service sectors to code obligations. Therefore, in the GATT, flexibility may be needed in the range of concessions that countries are able to offer. But notwithstanding these points, the U.S.–Canada agreement on services provides a valuable road map for GATT negotiators. To that end, it should lead over time to further liberalization of service markets around the world, and that will rebound to the benefit of firms in both the United States and Canada.

4

G. Firman Bentley _____

Perspective of a Multinational Firm

My perspective is that of a Canadian multinational firm. I believe that one must look at the world as Marshall McLuhan did: "It is truly a global village." Two years ago, Peter Drucker wrote in *Foreign Affairs* that economic dynamics have decisively shifted from the national economy to the world economy. This observation led him to state, "Any national economy that wants to prosper will have to accept that it is the world economy that leads and that domestic economic policies will succeed only if they strengthen, or at least do not impair, the country's international position. A country, industry, or company that puts the preservation of blue-collar manufacturing jobs ahead of international competitiveness will soon have neither production nor jobs."

My own company, Polysar, a major international company that is Canadian-owned, is a strong advocate of Peter Drucker's views as expressed above. We were established in 1942 as a part of the wartime effort and have grown to be one of the world's largest manufacturers of synthetic rubber. In fact, Polysar introduced synthetic rubber to the world at large immediately after the war when it was apparent that export markets were essential for the company's survival. The limited size of the Canadian domestic market and the postwar resurgence of natural rubber production required us to develop overseas markets for a number of our products in order to maximize the efficiency of our production facilities. This, in turn, led to the establishment of research and development facilities and additional production sites to service the burgeoning demands of the 1960s. If we had not traded internationally, particularly with the United States, we would not have survived. Thus, we learned our lesson very early.

Throughout this period, we have fought against trade barriers wherever we have found them and have been particularly concerned about the protectionist sentiment that has been building in the United States. This concern prompted us to support the free trade negotiations recently concluded between Canada and the United States. The resulting agreement provides better and fairer rules governing our trade and a dispute settlement procedure to resolve our differences.

It has been pointed out that Canada and the United States are each other's largest trading partners. In fact, merchandise trade between our two countries was $158 billion (U.S.) in 1988. The United States has been very concerned about its trade deficit, which has been growing throughout the 1980s. Canadian exports were growing throughout that period, and while our exports to the rest of the world were growing by 17 percent, U.S. exports to Canada were growing by 46 percent.

We truly are the United States' best customer. Other than Canada as a whole, the province of Ontario is the United States' largest trading partner, bigger than Japan. The state of Michigan is Canada's second largest trading partner after only the entire United States. In fact, the United States exports more to the 9 million people of Ontario than to the 200 million people of Great Britain, France, Germany, Belgium and Holland, the five founding countries of the European Economic Community. While there is a lot of talk in the United States about the importance of trade with Japan, not much is heard about trade with Canada. However, Canada is the United States' best trading partner and its second-best trading partner is the province of Ontario.

Polysar's largest manufacturing facilities are in southwestern Ontario, an area sometimes considered "geographically disadvantaged," located as it is in the north. However, consider a North American free trade zone (Figure 2). A circle drawn around southwestern Ontario shows unobstructed *same-day* access to a huge North American market which includes 54 percent of the U.S. payroll, 48 percent of its retail sales, and 54 percent of its manufacturing activity. Manufacturers in Detroit will have same-day access to 65 percent of Canadian economic activity and all the attendant manufacturing, retailing, and the like. Similar north-south trade flows between New York and Quebec and the Maritime provinces and New England will be enhanced.

This geographic fact is particularly significant in the context of just-in-time inventories, meaning that goods can be produced in a plant and delivered to a customer's loading dock on the same day. Places within that 500-mile radius are within one day's trucking distance from Sarnia, Ontario. This region includes northern New York, southeastern Ontario, and the entire eastern Great Lakes region. This location is a real advantage.

The compelling logic of the case for free trade is hardly new. Indeed, the matter was first discussed by Adam Smith in 1776 in his book *The Wealth of Nations.* We know from economists and our own experience that countries and businesses alike do better when they trade and do worse when they run into barriers. It is a myth that protected industries can grow and flourish behind the wall of protection, as has been said in Canada. For example, it is revealing to compare job creation in Canadian industries that have protective tariffs with those that do not. Table 12 shows changes in Canadian employment in selected industries from 1974 to 1982. The transportation equipment sector has created more jobs than any other, and it has no tariffs whatsoever. The chemical industry has also created more jobs than industries with greater tariff protection. The ones with the highest protection and tariffs have the worst job creation record of all. People who say that the Canada–U.S. Free Trade Agreement will hurt Canadian industries are, I think, mistaken. Double-digit tariff protection leads to incentives for labor and capital to remain in inefficient industries, higher costs to consumers, less choice available to consumers, and, in fact, loss of jobs overall.

My message is very simple. I believe we need to look outside our borders. There is no escape: a company's prosperity depends on trade and that fact places it squarely in today's global marketplace. We face a constant challenge to renew our products and production systems in order to meet the pressures of international competition. We can have free trade between our two countries and we can make this agreement a model for multilateral negotiations. Protectionism does not work. It leads, in the end, to contraction of jobs and protection of inefficient industries. Free trade works, and we should support it in both of our countries.

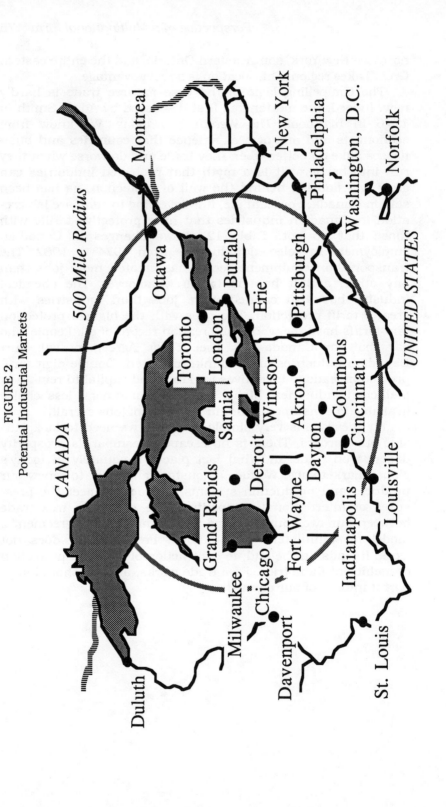

FIGURE 2
Potential Industrial Markets

500 Mile Radius

CANADA

UNITED STATES

Duluth
Milwaukee
Chicago
Davenport
Grand Rapids
Detroit
Fort Wayne
Windsor
Indianapolis
Dayton
Akron
Cincinnati
Columbus
St. Louis
Louisville
Sarnia
London
Toronto
Erie
Pittsburgh
Buffalo
Ottawa
Montreal
New York
Philadelphia
Washington, D.C.
Norfolk

TABLE 12
Canadian Employment, 1974-1982

Industry	Tariffs	Net Job Change
Transportation equip.	0	+37,977
Chemicals	5-9%	+8,615
Furniture	12.5%	-3,348
Textiles	20%	-4,097
Knitting mills	20%	-4,124
Clothing	22.5%	-10,358

SOURCE: Canadian Government—Department of Regional Industrial
      Expansion (DRIE)

5

Thomas A. Cronin _____

The Interrelationship of Canada, the United States, and the European Economic Community

The Clinton County Area Development Corporation has for some time been concerned about efforts to protect national prerogatives which might seriously dilute the potential economic opportunities that we see resulting from the Canada–U.S. Free Trade Agreement. We are fearful that analyzing the consequences for both the United States and Canada without considering very important and rapidly changing world conditions would leave the flanks of both nations exposed to foreign economic onslaughts.

This is particularly true, we believe, in terms of the European Community and its proposed radical changes to be implemented in 1992. The United States and Canada have a combined population of about 270 million with a gross domestic product of $5 trillion (U.S.). The European Community has about 320 million people which—if combined with the European Free Trade Association consisting of Austria, Finland, Norway, Sweden, and Switzerland—would currently generate $4.5 trillion in gross domestic product with a combined population of 335 million.

After reviewing 500 years of economic and military history, Paul Kennedy states in his epilogue to *The Rise and Fall of the World's Greatest Powers* that "The pattern of world politics looks roughly as follows: First, there will be a shift in both the share of total world power and total military spending from the five largest concentrations of strength to many more nations; but that will be a gradual process and no other state is likely to join the present pentarchy of the United States, the USSR, China, Japan and the European Community in the near future."

This observation is particularly significant because national states are normally identified as being the economic, military, and political forces that shape the international scene.

Instead, Kennedy suggests that the European Community will strengthen its role in world economic affairs and perhaps eventually in military and political affairs as well. Indeed, President Gorbachev of the Soviet Union has proposed that western and eastern Europe become "one European house" stretching from the Urals to the Atlantic.

Changes in economic and strategic strength cannot be measured by each nation independent of events in a volatile world; they can only be measured in relation to what other nations are doing to improve their economic and military strength and to build political coalitions. All of this suggests that Canada and the United States should watch closely world events that shape relative economic, military, and political positions, particularly the elimination of trade barriers by 1992 among member nations of the European Community, the development of the European Parliament, and political developments in eastern Europe.

On the other side of the world, we have witnessed Japan and the manner in which that nation has ascended steadily even after withstanding a brutal defeat in World War II. On the Asiatic mainland, we are witnessing the emergence of the People's Republic of China from a long period of counterproductive isolation. China has more than one billion people, or roughly one-fifth of the entire world's population. Most observers feel that the emergence of China to its full potential will take a very long time, but that it possesses the potential to grow very quickly. With the help of the United States and Canada, that pace could be accelerated; however, that help must be mutually beneficial to the participants and based on a strong sense of national security within each cooperating state.

The United States and Canada have substantial boundaries on both the Atlantic and the Pacific Oceans and most observers feel that the Pacific basin will be the economic dynamo of the next generation. An association of Southeast Asian nations represents an oriental counterpart to the European Community. What is the relative strength or weakness of the United States and Canada with respect to both the Atlantic and Asian frontiers?

We have witnessed the growth of Japan, Taiwan, South Korea, Hong Kong, and Singapore and the way they have eroded the growth rate of manufacturing in the United States and Canada. What would happen if military power were to follow the expected economic growth? We see a continuing dynamism in the Pacific Rim. In 1960 the Asian Pacific countries had 7.8 percent of the world's gross domestic product; by 1982, this figure had more than doubled to 16.4 percent.

Across the Atlantic, a confederation is being formed that will combine many of the strengths and presumably eliminate many of the weaknesses that Europe has suffered since before the era of Christianity. The dynamics of economic, military, and political strength are bound to influence any bilateral agreement such as the Canada-U.S. Free Trade Agreement.

Decision makers in Ottawa and Washington will have very little influence on those making decisions in either Tokyo, Bonn, Brussels, or Beijing. Therefore, we must anticipate what the consequences of these developments might be for international trade and efforts to preserve peace. The Canada-U.S. Free Trade Agreement may bring growth and prosperity to North America and there is little doubt that the United States and Canada will both be stronger by virtue of the proposed agreement. However, this will only be relative to the events taking place in Europe and the Pacific basin and indeed in many other parts of the world.

PART II

TRADE AND ECONOMIC OPPORTUNITIES IN THE ST. LAWRENCE RIVER BASIN REGION

6

DANIEL B. WALSH _____

Perspective of the New York State
Business Council

I represent the business community in New York as president
of the Business Council of New York State. We represent the
real breadth of industry in New York State, both large and
small, from Lake Ontario to the tip of Montauk Point and from
the borders of the great nation of Canada down to the southern boundary with New Jersey. I will present some of the business community's opinions about the Canada–U.S. Free Trade
Agreement (FTA) as looked upon in New York State.

The view of the business community could probably be
summed up in two sentences. We are very delighted with the
close, mutually beneficial economic relationship that we have
with Canada now. We look forward to even more benefits for
both sides under the Canada–U.S. Free Trade Agreement. To
elaborate on those two points is not hard because talking
about Canada is a pleasure for a New Yorker who, until about
a year ago, was able to get into downtown Toronto in less than
two hours.

New Yorkers do not think of Canadians as "new" neighbors.
We have known them for generations and we like who we
know. In fact, one of the most interesting sidelights of the free
trade process over the last two years has been our growing
awareness of just how close our two peoples and our two
economies have become even without a rational and comprehensive trade agreement between us. That is a triumph of the
hardworking spirit of our peoples and of the good business
sense which prevails on both sides of the border over the
vagaries of the political process. In that sense, the Canada–
U.S. Free Trade Agreement really just ratifies what our peoples
and our businesses have already achieved: a strong and mutually dependent relationship.

New York State has the good fortune to share a border with
Canada, and our companies and our people derive great bene-

fits from that fact. As of 1988, Canadian-owned companies employed over 50,000 New Yorkers, a figure that had almost doubled in ten years. Overall, Canadian companies have over $5 billion invested in New York. Some two million Canadian visitors spend an estimated $220 million in New York each year. Let me extend a personal invitation to the other 24 million Canadians who have not had that privilege. Direct exports into Canada support some 132,000 jobs in New York State, including about 70,000 manufacturing jobs. Canada supplies 11 percent of our electrical energy. Perhaps even more important than those statistics is the spirit of our relationship. Our people and our businesses are open to each other and proud of it.

The Business Council's membership includes over 100 of the Fortune 500 business firms, as well as thousands of other large and small businesses across New York State. Our companies, large and small, have told me that they are absolutely excited about the prospects under the FTA. The manufacturers who are already active in Canada see it as an opportunity to become even more so. There is great interest in the provisions which will reduce barriers in the service industries, in finance, and in energy. And we know that as trade expands between our two countries, New York is in a kind of gateway position. As Canada grows, we grow. Multinational companies welcome the opportunities provided by the agreement. They expect any adjustments to be relatively minor and temporary, and they expect both sides to gain in the long run.

However, what is really exciting about the growing trade relationship between the United States and Canada is not the impact on the multinationals, the companies from both countries already operating on both sides of the border. It is about creating more multinationals, involving more and more companies of all sizes and all kinds in growth and investment and new ventures and progress in both countries. The multinationals we should be concerned with are not the ones that are in place now. The ones to consider are those that would never be in place if we do not make a concerted effort to bring down the trade barriers between us.

I am a strong believer in free trade. I think history shows that free trade is a "win-win" situation for both parties. History also shows that in a free trade relationship, the partner with the most to gain is the one that will gain improved access to the larger market. In this situation, that country is obviously Canada because the U.S. market is ten times larger. But our

New York companies are not looking at this as some kind of a balance sheet where both parties must realize equal gains. What interests us is the dynamics of the process of free trade and international competition. That dynamic process, I think, is the key to why this new relationship is so important and valuable to both countries. A more open trading relationship between the United States and Canada will help companies in both our countries train themselves for the much more difficult economic struggles that we both confront outside the North American continent.

Canadian companies must learn to compete in the United States. It has been said that if they cannot compete in that market, they cannot compete anywhere. We in the United States must also remember that exactly the same thing is true of us in facing Canadian markets. If we cannot compete in Canada—with whom we share so much of a common business culture—we are never going to be able to compete in Japan or South Korea or Europe.

Our close relationship gives companies in both our countries a chance to get accustomed to conducting business in a global economy. That is already happening with hundreds upon hundreds of medium-sized and smaller firms on both sides of the border, and that trend will accelerate under the Canada–U.S. Free Trade Agreement. John Crosbie, Canada's trade minister, recently said something that captured the new entrepreneurial competitive spirit that is enlivening both our economies—a spirit that will redouble as our relationship strengthens: "There isn't an American I've seen that I'm afraid of, with the exception of maybe Hulk Hogan and Mike Tyson."

I know what he means. American business also has no fear going into this new relationship, but maybe we ought to phrase it a little differently: "There isn't a Canadian we've seen with whom we didn't want to do business, so let's get on with it."

7

PREM GANDHI _____

Trade and Investment Flows in
New York State: Effects of the
Free Trade Agreement

Before discussing the effect of free trade on New York State, let me make a few general comments, starting with the Canada–U.S. Free Trade Agreement (FTA) itself. The FTA is a closed deal between the United States and Canada. This means that it is a bilateral agreement to eliminate over the next ten years tariff and nontariff barriers to trade in goods and services between these two countries. Each country will continue to maintain its external tariffs with other nations. By limiting the tariff reductions to each other, both countries must insure that no other country can take advantage of the regional market by entering via the low tariff country. The implication is that customs officials will have to be extremely careful about the agreement's provisions regarding the rules of origin in order to prevent other countries from using the back door to enter our markets.

Much has been written about who gained and who lost in the process of negotiating this agreement. The fact of the matter is that both countries have lost and both have gained. Compromises were made by both countries in order to reach agreement. For example, the United States has gained through provisions regarding trade in energy and services and through the relaxation of investment restrictions in Canada. Canada's greatest gain has been in securing access to the world's largest and wealthiest market. Canada's ability to keep its cultural industries protected and the establishment of a dispute settlement framework are also generally considered important gains to Canada.

What does free trade mean for New York State? Regional economists point to the strategic location of the state on the U.S.–Canadian border in analyzing the economic effects. New York is located next to the most populous region and most prosperous provinces in Canada, namely Ontario and Quebec. The industrial heartland of Canada is located in these two provinces: almost 70 percent of the total market of Canada lies there. The two major cities in Canada—Toronto and Montreal—contain 74 percent of manufacturing revenues and 72 percent of Canadian and foreign assets. Three-fourths of Canada's major corporations and multinational firms are located in these two cities.

The proximity of Canada to New York State has been responsible for forging economic relations which are already extremely strong, as will be evident from the data presented below. Any aspiring businessperson who wants to talk about the effect of free trade on New York State must remember the importance of this location. Quebec and Ontario are also two provinces that are likely to gain the most with free trade. In spite of some opposition to the agreement in Ontario, the fact of the matter is that once the adjustments have been made, Ontario will be the province that will gain the most from freer trade. Thus, at the macro level, New York State is well poised to take advantage of the agreement, given its diversified economy in manufacturing, services (especially the financial sector), agriculture, and tourism.

Location is also important at the micro level. There really are two different orientations in New York State. One is the northern orientation—north of Albany, Schenectady, Utica, and Syracuse. The other orientation looks southward. We have a Canadian orientation in the northern part of the state. Canada has heavily invested in New York State, particularly the six counties of northern New York. Canada also has contributed significantly in retail trade and tourism expenditures in the northern area. The Canadian orientation in northern New York will be strengthened with the FTA. The southern orientation differs because downstate is really more a part of the industrial heartland of the United States. Under pre-FTA tariff barriers, northern New York has not been fully integrated with Canada. With trade and investment barriers reduced, northern New York will be in a particularly advantageous position between two industrial heartlands. One is in the north, extending from Quebec City through Montreal, Ottawa, and Toronto to Windsor. The other is further south, from Boston and New York to Chicago. Thus, the effects of free trade will be particularly important in this northern New York region because of its location and northern orientation.

The potential benefits of free trade to New York State can be appreciated by reviewing some bilateral trade statistics. In 1988, total exports to Canada accounted for about 23 percent of all U.S. exports, and these products accounted for almost 70 percent of Canadian imports. By the same token, about 75 percent of Canadian exports came to the United States, comprising 19 percent of all United States imports. There is nothing surprising about this situation because these two economies are highly integrated. Almost 56 percent of all trade between the United States and Canada is through intrafirm purchases by firms operating on both sides of the border. Furthermore, almost 75 percent of U.S.–Canadian trade is already duty free and very low tariffs exist on the remaining 25 percent. Tables 13 and 14 highlight these bilateral trade flows.

Because New York State is adjacent to Quebec and Ontario, it is important to examine each province's contribution to trade between the United States and Canada. Recently, 85 percent of U.S. exports to Canada went to these two provinces, while 73 percent of United States imports from Canada originated in Quebec and Ontario. In New York State, the importance of Ontario and Quebec is even more magnified. In 1988, 96 percent of New York's Canadian exports went to Quebec and Ontario, and 90 percent of New York's Canadian imports came from those two provinces. New York is Quebec's largest customer, taking about 20 percent of Quebec's exports to the United States, and is Ontario's second largest customer, buying 18 percent of its exports to the United States. It is also important to note that almost 50 percent of *total* New York exports go to Canada, and this percentage is increasing. These exports support approximately 132,000 jobs in the state.

Lately, concerns have been expressed regarding the declining relative share of New York State's exports to Canada, from 12 percent of total U.S. exports in 1980 to about 8 percent in 1988. However, much of the decline can be attributed to changes in the value of the U.S. dollar relative to the Canadian dollar and the changing structure of the New York State economy from manufacturing toward services.

Table 15 lists the ten leading commodities traded between New York State and Canada. It is notable that several products are traded both ways, again evidence of the complementarity of the economic structures of New York, Ontario, and Quebec, and of the close integration of the two countries. But the trade flows also suggest that New York State has a competitive advantage in certain products—computers, auto parts, electronic tubes and semiconductors, photographic goods, and printed matter. New York State will not lose its competitive advantage in these products with the FTA; in fact, if anything, freer trade will strengthen New York's competitive advantage. Tables 16 indicates the values, sources, and destinations of products that are traded between New York State and Canada.

Financial and investment capital also flows between Canada and New York State. In fact, in 1987 the total value of foreign direct investment in New York State was over $22.5 billion. The largest portion of that investment, 23 percent or $5.2 billion, came from Canada. Certain regions in New York State, including northern New York, have benefited greatly from Canadian investment. In a 1985 study, we found that 60 percent of all Canadian companies located in New York State came from Ontario and at least 35 percent came from Quebec. There are approximately 180–200 Canadian companies located in New York State and they provide about 50,000 jobs to New Yorkers. While they are located in all regions of the state, they are mostly concentrated in two areas, northern New York and western New York.

Earlier research that I conducted indicated reasons why Canadian businesses locate in New York (Gandhi, 1985). The results are shown in Table 17. Canadian investors consider New York State a gateway to the rich U.S. market. While tariffs might, in theory, be an important consideration in investment decisions, Canadian companies consider the size of the U.S. market and the potential for growth as more important reasons. They have located plants in northern New York and western New York for proximity to head offices which are located either in Montreal or Toronto. The only other extremely important factor is transportation, both for the ease of moving goods and for facilitating travel by company executives who commute between their operations in New York State and their head offices in Canada. All other location factors seem to be less important.

How would New York fare under freer trade? To my knowledge, no quantitative study has been conducted to estimate exactly what will happen to New York State. We can, however, develop a framework based upon the knowledge, precedents, and historical experience here and elsewhere in the world about the effect of free trade. This framework suggests that two effects will happen immediately. First, when resources now being imported from Canada become duty free in the U.S. market, costs of production and, in turn, prices for New York State products should fall. Second, the removal of Canadian tariffs, which are twice as high as U.S. tariffs, will encourage products to move northward into the Canadian market.

Table 18 lists present tariffs by industrial sector. The historical experiences of the European Free Trade Association (EFTA) and the European Community (EC) suggest that products currently being traded are not the only ones that will benefit from free trade. Tariff reduction and a vibrant Canadian economy will mean *new* products and *new* trade in areas where currently none exist. In fact, in the experience of the EC, the dynamic effects of trade liberalization far outweighed the immediate benefits of trade expansion. Additionally, removal of impediments to services trade should be welcomed by New York State because of its competitive advantage. The service sector is labor-intensive and people-oriented, and therefore, the expansion of trade in services should mean more and better-paying jobs in New York.

The effects of free trade are less certain in terms of Canadian investment in New York State. Our study of factors that affect location suggests that tariffs have not been an important factor influencing Canadian investment south of the border (Gandhi, 1985). An informal poll conducted in Clinton County suggests that there will be no change in the inflow of capital resulting from the FTA (Gandhi, 1989). However, free trade will create a huge market in North America where every region, every state, and every province will have to compete in order to attract investment. The FTA also aims to relax investment barriers between United States and Canada. There will be pressure at state, regional, and provincial levels to make the investment climate more attractive by reducing impediments to the free flow of capital. In the past, Canadian companies were more concerned about their access to the U.S. market. Free trade will change the relative importance of this factor. The challenge for New York State businesses and policy-makers is to insure that the state's existing competitive advantages are maintained.

TABLE 13
U.S. Exports to Canada, 1988
(million U.S. dollars)

	Quebec	Ontario	Total
Live animals	8.9	60.6	88.6
Food, beverages, feed, and tobacco	551.0	1,837.3	3,485.0
Inedible crude materials	558.0	1,848.5	2,746.4
Inedible fabricated materials	1,902.0	9,347.7	13,365.4
Total end products, inedible	6,776.7	43,019.2	52,313.4
Industrial machinery	707.2	4,134.2	6,209.6
Agricultural machinery	66.2	487.4	1,118.9
Transportation equipment	2,341.8	21,127.8	26,575.5
Other equipment & tools	1,985.5	10,066.0	13,669.8
Other end products	558.2	3,457.5	4,739.6
Special transactions	290.9	1,055.0	1,760.2
Total Exports to Canada	8,969.7	53,422.0	73,705.0
From New York	1,012.7	4,392.5	5,699.0

SOURCE: Statistics Canada

TABLE 14
Canada's Exports to U.S., 1988
(million U.S. dollars)

	Quebec	Ontario	Total
Live animals	9.9	79.7	451.3
Food, beverages, feed, and tobacco	497.1	905.0	3,115.1
Inedible crude materials	523.9	623.1	7,372.0
Inedible fabricated materials	7,152.9	9,790.1	26,751.3
Total end products, inedible	5,086.8	34,262.9	41,385.2
Industrial machinery	304.6	1,788.1	2,352.2
Agricultural machinery	20.2	353.2	517.9
Transportation equipment	2,693.8	27,057.2	30,497.1
Other equipment & tools	1,284.7	3,484.2	5,341.9
Other end products	783.5	1,580.2	2,676.1
Special transactions	162.6	183.1	470.2
Total Exports to U.S.	13,433.2	45,843.9	79,546.0
To New York	2,531.3	8,316.1	12,227.4

SOURCE: Statistics Canada

TABLE 15
Ten Leading Exports and Imports of New York, 1988
(million U.S. dollars)

Exports to Canada	Value	Value	Imports from Canada
Motor vehicle parts (except engines)	416.4	3,960.3	Passenger automobiles and chassis
Telecommunication & related equipment	340.0	669.5	Aluminum, including alloys
Aluminum, including alloys	314.7	632.6	Precious metals, including alloys
Electronic computers	297.4	583.1	Newsprint paper
Electronic tubes & semiconductors	264.1	567.6	Trucks, truck tractors and chassis
Photographic goods	179.3	424.5	Natural gas
Metals in ores, concentrates, & scraps	177.8	296.9	Motor vehicle parts (except engines)
Books & pamphlets	118.8	264.9	Wood pulp & similar pulp
Newspapers, magazines, periodicals	110.6	253.1	Crude petroleum
Paper & paperboard	107.4	250.2	Photographic goods
Total of Ten	2,326.5	7,902.7	Total of Ten
Share of Total	40.8%	64.7%	Share of Total
Total to Canada	5,699.0	12,227.4	Total from Canada

SOURCE: Statistics Canada

TABLE 16
Sources and Destination of New York-Canada
Trade of Leading Products, 1988
(million U.S. dollars)

Product	N.Y. Exports	Destination	N.Y. Imports	Source
Vehicles & Parts				
Passenger automobiles and chassis	103.9	Ont. Que.	3,960.3	Ont. Que.
Motor vehicle parts, except engines	416.4	Ont. Que.	296.9	Ont. Que.
Truck, truck tractors and chassis	5.8	Ont. Prairies Que.	567.6	Ont. Que.
Engines & engine parts	131.3	Ont. Pacific Que.	26.7	Ont. Que.
Other motor vehicles	17.0	Ont. Que.	129.3	Que. Ont.
Aircraft engines, parts	56.4	Ont. Que.	22.0	Ont. Que.
Metals				
Aluminum, including alloys	314.7	Ont. Que.	669.5	Que. Ont.
Metals in ores, concentrates and scraps	177.8	Ont. Que.	0	
Precious metals, including alloys	70.5	Ont. Que.	632.6	Ont. Pacific
Equipment				
Telecommunication and related equipment	340.0	Ont. Que.	200.4	Que. Ont.
Electronic computers	297.4	Ont. Que.	0	
Electronic tubes & semiconductors	264.1	Ont. Que.	0	
Office machines and equipment	21.2	Ont. Que.	114.0	Ont. Que.

98

TABLE 16 (cont.)
Sources and Destination of New York-Canada
Trade of Leading Products, 1988
(million U.S. dollars)

Product	N.Y. Exports	Destination	N.Y. Imports	Source
Wood				
Newsprint paper	0		583.1	Que. Ont.
Wood pulp	9.5	Que. Ont.	264.9	Que. Atl.
Paper & paperboard	107.4	Ont. Que.	127.2	Ont. Que.
Lumber	50.5	Ont. Que.	200.0	Pacific, Que.
Energy				
Natural gas	0		424.5	Albt. Ont.
Crude petroleum	0		253.1	Albt.
Electricity	0		246.0	Ont. Que.
Petroleum & coal products	39.9	Ont. Que.	183.1	Ont. Que.
Photographic & printed goods				
Photographic goods	179.3	Ont. Que.	250.2	Ont. Que.
Books & pamphlets	118.8	Ont. Que.	0	
Newspapers, magazines, & periodicals	110.6	Ont. Pacific	0	
Printed matter	18.7	Ont. Que.	210.9	Ont. Que.

SOURCE: Statistics Canada

TABLE 17
Importance of Locational Factors to Canadian
Firms in New York

Factor	Percent Responding
Extremely Important (over 60 percent)	
Nearness to parent company	81
Potential for growth in U.S.	79
Location in the area	77
Transportation highways	64
Moderately Important (30-59 percent)	
Nearness to customers in U.S.	39
Trainable labor	39
U.S.-Canadian tariff	34
Skilled labor	32
Somewhat Important (less than 30 percent)	
Community attitude	29
Airways	24
New York State incentives	24
Existing industrial base	24
Local incentives	20
Public infrastructure	18
Banking restrictions	16
Low electric rates	15
Potential for exports from U.S.	15
Railways	9
Raw materials	8
Special facilities for foreign trade	5
Cultural amenities	3.3
Seaways	2

SOURCE: Gandhi, Prem. "Canadian Investment in New York:
Appalachia or Haven for Foreign Investment?" Special
Report #9. Albany: Rockefeller Institute, 1985.

TABLE 18
Tariffs by Industrial Sector, Post-Tokyo Round, 1987
(ad valorem)

Industry	Canada	United States
Textiles	16.9	7.2
Clothing	23.7	18.4
Leather products	4.0	2.5
Footwear	21.5	9.0
Wood products	2.5	0.2
Furniture and fixtures	14.3	4.6
Paper products	6.6	0.0
Printing and publishing	1.1	0.3
Chemicals	7.9	0.6
Petroleum products	0.4	0.0
Rubber products	7.3	3.2
Nonmetal mineral products	4.4	0.3
Glass products	6.9	5.7
Iron and steel	5.1	2.7
Nonferrous metals	3.3	0.5
Metal products	8.6	4.0
Nonelectrical machinery	4.6	2.2
Electrical machinery	7.5	4.5
Transportation equipment	0.0	0.0
Miscellaneous manufactures	5.0	0.9

NOTE: Canadian tariff averages are weighted by imports from the United States and vice versa.

SOURCE: Office of the United States Special Trade Representative

8

RICHARD M. MCGAHEY AND JONATHAN P. DOH _____

Effects of Freer Trade on New York State: Economic Impact and Policy Considerations

The Canada–United States Free Trade Agreement (FTA) is a significant milestone in the trading relationship between the two nations. While the forecasted effects of the FTA on New York State's economy have yet to be studied using highly detailed econometric analyses, it is clear that many industries and regions of the state will benefit. For the state as a whole, however, we expect that the benefits will be modest, especially when compared to the effects of other important economic phenomena such as business cycle fluctuations or changes in currency exchange rates.

This chapter presents information on the FTA and its potential impact on New York. The first section provides pertinent Canadian trade and investment data for New York. We then outline the anticipated impact of the FTA on the New York State economy, focusing on the specific industries and regions that stand to benefit from increased trade. We also consider the likely impact of the FTA on cross-border investment. The chapter concludes with a brief discussion of policies that have been or will be implemented to help New York businesses take full advantage of emerging economic opportunities resulting from the FTA.

TRADE AND INVESTMENT BETWEEN CANADA AND NEW YORK

The U.S. merchandise trade deficit with Canada grew throughout the 1980s, as shown in Figure 3. For much of the decade, Canada's commodity exports to the United States have been increasing at a faster rate than U.S. exports to Canada. New York State accounted for 8.6 percent of U.S. commodity trade with Canada in 1988, but New York's trade gap with Canada (Figure 4) widened even more than the corresponding national trade deficit. New York's imports from Canada are a rising share of the U.S. total and the state's exports to Canada are a declining share of the U.S. total. However, this gap may

101

be overstated because some goods that enter New York from Canada are destined for other locations. This caveat applies to valuation and trade-balance figures.

Three trends should be noted. First, overall U.S.–Canada trade has increased dramatically during the 1980s. Second, Canada has enjoyed a bilateral commodity trade surplus with the United States throughout the 1980s. At the same time, New York's deficit has been widening slightly faster than has the U.S. trade gap.

However, this trend in merchandise trade has been offset by trends in services trade across the border. By 1988, U.S. services trade with Canada had grown to $25.5 billion in exports and $11.2 billion in imports. Combining goods and services, the U.S. bilateral current account deficit has been narrowing over the last several years and, in fact, showed a $3.4 billion surplus in 1988. While services trade figures are not compiled state by state, New York's unique concentration of "exportable" services in sectors like law, accounting, design engineering, management consulting and, of course, financial services, suggests that at least one quarter of the U.S. production of services exports can be plausibly attributed to New York firms.

New York's commodity trade with Canada is largely comprised of inedible end products. The leading exports from New York to Canada in 1988, shown in Figure 5, were motor vehicle parts and engines, other telecommunications equipment, aluminum, computers, electronic tubes and semiconductors, and photographic goods. A large share of these commodities can be classified as "high-technology" products. Figure 6 indicates that Canadian shipments to New York are primarily autos, wood pulp and newsprint, aluminum, precious metals, trucks, and natural gas.

In addition to commodity and services trade, Canadian and U.S. firms also engage in significant cross-border investment. In 1988, Canada was by far the leading country of origin for foreign direct investment in New York, accounting for nearly one quarter of foreign direct investment in the state (Figures 7 and 8).* There has been a steady increase in the absolute value of Canadian direct investment in New York and it is expected that

---

*Editors' footnote: These numbers represent the value of total fixed assets (gross plant, property, and equipment) under control of a foreign partner. Calculation of foreign direct investment in this manner permits disaggregated analysis by state.

Canada will remain a leading source of foreign investment in the state. Figure 9 shows that between 1981 and 1988 the gross book value of property, plant, and equipment under Canadian control in New York rose steadily. The jump in 1986 and 1987 may be largely attributed to the Campeau takeover of Allied Stores in 1986 and Federated Department Stores in 1987.

Figure 10 shows the total value of foreign direct investment from all sources relative to Canadian investment in New York. The total value of foreign investment from sources other than Canada has increased at a slightly faster rate, but Canadian direct investment still accounts for the largest single share. It is likely that much of this direct investment and bilateral trade represents intrafirm transfers between branch locations or affiliates of firms that conduct business on both sides of the border. While the total number of Canadian-owned affiliates in New York has dropped slightly in the period 1981–1988 (Figure 11), the total employment of these affiliates rose (Figure 12), suggesting that their average size is growing.

This perhaps reflects a more permanent commitment of Canadian firms to expanding their New York operations. Empirical research suggests that Canadian investment may have more beneficial income and employment effects than direct investment from other countries because Canadian investment tends to be "greenfield". Harrington and Barnas (1987) found that in upstate New York regions, "Canadian investment was overwhelmingly via new firms . . . compared with . . . foreign investment overall" (p. 16). Prior to the FTA, Canada already was a major source of investment and employment in New York and we expect these trends to continue.

IMPACT OF THE FTA

Preliminary analysis indicates that many industries and regions in New York will benefit from the FTA. However, the overall effect will be relatively small when compared with the impact on the state's economy of other underlying factors such as the overall business cycle, movements in interest rates, and competitive pressures in financial services and manufacturing. Nevertheless, the economic impact of the FTA on New York will be greater than on many other states, given our proximity to Canadian economic and population centers and the relatively large volume of bilateral trade and investment.

Three reasons account for our scenario of modest short-run effects for most New York State regions and industries.

First is the enormous size of the United States and New York markets relative to Canada. The U.S. economy is over ten times the size of Canada's and the annual output of New York alone is roughly that of Canada. The FTA is likely to have much more impact on Canada because of this relative size differential. Second, positive effects probably will not be dramatic because trade already flows relatively freely between the two countries. Over 70 percent of traded goods crossed between the United States and Canada duty free prior to the implementation of the FTA. The third factor is that the elimination of tariffs with the FTA will be a gradual process and it will take time to establish new trade and investment patterns. Of course, regions of the state along the border with Canada are likely to be most affected by the FTA.

Notwithstanding the above, small manufacturers in New York should be particularly well positioned under the agreement for several reasons. First, more Canadian government contracts have become open for American firms as the threshold value for competitive bidding falls from $171,000 to $25,000. This will result in more government procurement opportunities for smaller firms. Second, unlike some large American firms, many small plants still have economies of scale that can be exploited as they increase production and reduce unit costs by servicing the expanded marketplace. This extension of production runs and specialization could result in expanded market sales and generate increased employment and income.

Third, and perhaps most important, many small manufacturing firms are currently not accustomed to exporting. Canadian trade is an excellent opportunity for introducing New York firms to the export market because of the cultural similarities and the long standing tradition of bilateral trade. One estimate suggests that although only about 10 percent of small firms now export actively, as many as 75 percent produce a product similar to one currently being sold in foreign markets. Expanded economic opportunities with Canada will not only be beneficial in and of themselves, but could be an excellent laboratory and testing ground for American firms to develop an international orientation.

Industries such as finance, publishing, telecommunications, and electronics that were previously faced with tariff or nontariff restrictions are well positioned to take advantage of the opening of Canadian markets. Canadian tariffs on some of New York's most competitive commodities, including data processors, satellites, telephone sets, electronics and electronic machinery, printed matter, and photographic equipment and supplies will be eliminated under the FTA. Financial services, a major growth industry in the state, will have even greater opportunities with the expansion of the Canadian market and the decentralization of back office and other data processing activities away from the New York City area.

With lower U.S. tariffs on Canadian goods, Canadian firms will have more access to New York markets. Some rationalization of New York's economy may occur as formerly protected industries meet increased competition, particularly in agriculture, forest products, and other raw materials industries. However, it is important to note that Canadian tariffs on average are more than twice those of the United States. For many of the commodities cited above, Canadian tariffs prior to the FTA were even higher. Thus, in most sectors, U.S. and New York firms should be able to compete very effectively.

High-technology manufacturing products provide perhaps the most significant opportunities for growth in New York exports to Canada. The demand for high-technology products is projected to remain strong, and New York holds a competitive advantage in the production of many of these goods. Canadian tariffs and nontariff barriers on these products are high, so special price advantages should accrue to New York products as tariffs are removed. For example, Canadian tariffs on data and word processors of 3.9 percent were to be eliminated in January 1989 as were duties on satellites and telephone sets, which had tariffs of 10.3 and 17.5 percent, respectively. The 4 percent duty on semiconductors and the 10.2 to 17.8 percent tariff on telecommunications equipment will also be phased out under the FTA. The photographic equipment and supplies industry, one of New York's most important manufacturing sectors, should benefit from the elimination of a 10.2 percent Canadian tariff on color and instant print film, a 9.2 percent tariff on photo plates, and the removal of tariffs on a variety of other optical and photographic goods.

The travel and tourism industry in New York also should be among the beneficiaries of the FTA. Some of the effects will be immediate, while some will occur over a longer period of time. More effective advertisement of tourist locations and services will be available in Canada as tariff and nontariff barriers on U.S. travel information are removed. Also, Canadian shoppers traveling to New York will no longer pay duties on clothing and other consumer goods when reentering Canada if goods meet the 50 percent North American content rule. (Of course, Canadians will continue to pay excise, sales, and other taxes.) Finally, liberalized regulations concerning temporary entry of business persons may mean more business-related travel by Canadians to New York and greater use of the state's convention facilities and regional airports.

While the FTA provides an improved climate for New York exports in agriculture and natural resources, many of the most egregious distortions to agricultural trade were not addressed by the agreement. For example, both the Canadian dairy supply management scheme and the U.S. dairy price support program were left intact. Moreover, ice cream and yogurt, currently dutiable in Canada at around 15 percent, were added to the Canadian import control list. This means that the Canadian Dairy Commission must issue a license for importation of these goods. It had been hoped that New York could gain increased sales of these dairy-processing industry products. However, a recent GATT ruling found that the import control procedures constitute a nontariff barrier, and Canada may yet be required to liberalize these practices.

Foreign direct investment is an issue of major interest to New Yorkers. Canadian investment in new facilities, acquisitions, and joint ventures has been instrumental in improving the economic climate in some regions, especially in border areas. Canadian investment also has resulted in the occasional retooling or reopening of a dormant manufacturing plant, or the reemployment of displaced workers (as occurred recently in Rouses Point).

There has been concern that the reduction of tariff barriers will result in less incentive for Canadians to invest in New York. However, most of the analysis of location decisions by Canadian manufacturing and service firms indicates that tariffs are only one factor, and sometimes a relatively minor one, in a very complex decision process (Gandhi, 1986). Firms seek market information, proximity to consumers, and labor availability, as well as tariff avoidance. Tariffs are not irrelevant, but they certainly are not the most important factor in location decisions. Thus, we conclude that the prospects for continued Canadian direct investment in New York State are quite strong as Canadian firms seek a market foothold and higher worker productivity. The lowering of tariff barriers by themselves should not significantly inhibit new investments.

Because of its close geographic proximity to Canada, the St. Lawrence River valley will be one of the regions of the state most affected by the FTA. There will be emerging opportunities in the St. Lawrence valley region for small manufacturing firms, as well as for distribution and warehousing facilities. Continued investment by Canadian firms will stimulate the economic base in the region as a whole.

The western New York region surrounding Buffalo also should benefit. Because of considerable tourism, customs, shipping, warehousing, distribution and direct investment activity, the effects of the FTA will be felt strongly here. This region is advantageously located between the wealthiest and most developed provinces in Canada and the eastern seaboard of the United States.

STATE POLICY AND THE FTA

Opportunities exist for additional New York involvement in bilateral trade and investment. There are a variety of programs and efforts that the state, in cooperation with local development groups, can implement to help firms take advantage of new opportunities created by the agreement. For instance, a new export trade demonstration project in the Department of Economic Development provides such support. One of the first grants under that program went to the Rochester Chamber of Commerce to promote the advantages of the FTA in that region. Development groups in other regions, including the Adirondack North Country Association and the North Country Alliance, have structured similar programs with the assistance of the State Department of Economic Development. The export trade projects program is part of the omnibus Economic Development Act of 1987, which created a number of new and innovative programs within the department.

New York has a number of additional initiatives to assist industries, individual firms, and economic development groups to take advantage of opportunities resulting from the FTA. Governor Cuomo has generally emphasized programs designed to make New York industries more competitive on a global scale, and Vincent Tese, the Director of Economic Development, is leading this effort. Additionally, Lieutenant Governor Lundine and members of the Department of Economic Development staff are working to expand subnational relationships at the provincial and state level.

It is important to note that New York State has a more

active presence in Canada than any other state. As other states scramble to establish offices in Canada, New York is entering its second quarter-century, with offices in Toronto and Montreal. Specific programs to help New York businesses take advantage of the agreement include regional education and training seminars to familiarize businesses with the FTA and its possible impact; planning grants for regional studies and regional impact analyses of the FTA; the Export Trade Demonstration project mentioned above; plans to link Canadian tourism with New York tourism in ways that can benefit this region; and the variety of programs that help New York State businesses in the areas of technology, financing, and training. As the Canada–U.S. Free Trade Agreement is implemented, the Department of Economic Development and other state agencies are eager to work with New York State businesses and with New York State's economic community to take full advantage of the economic opportunities it creates.

FIGURE 3
U.S. Merchandise Trade with Canada, 1980–1988

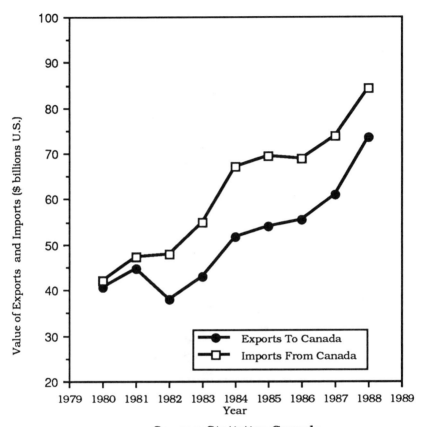

Source: Statistics Canada

FIGURE 4
New York State Merchandise Trade with Canada, 1980–1988

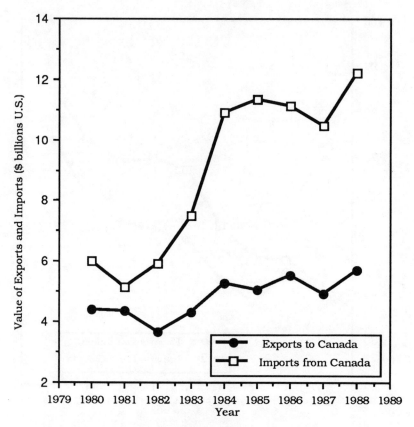

Source: Statistics Canada

111

FIGURE 5
Leading New York State Commodity Exports to Canada, 1988

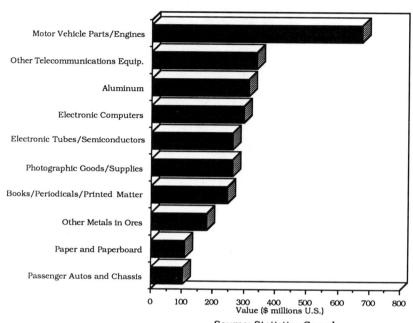

Source: Statistics Canada
Note: Commodities grouped according to authors' convention

112

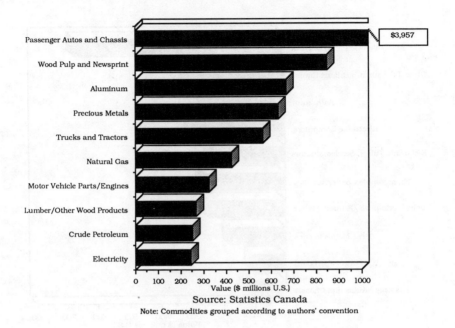

FIGURE 6
Leading New York State Commodity Imports from Canada, 1988

Source: Statistics Canada
Note: Commodities grouped according to authors' convention

FIGURE 7
Book Value of Foreign-owned Property, Plant, and Equipment in New
York State, by Leading Country of Origin, 1988 (billion U.S. dollars)

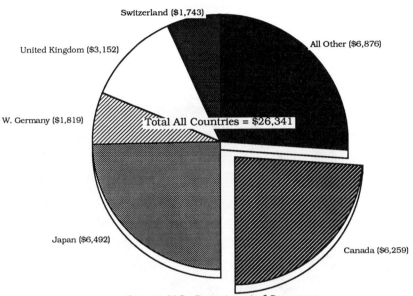

Switzerland ($1,743)

United Kingdom ($3,152)

All Other ($6,876)

W. Germany ($1,819)

Total All Countries = $26,341

Japan ($6,492)

Canada ($6,259)

Source: U.S. Department of Commerce,
Bureau of Economic Analysis

114

FIGURE 8
Book Value of Canadian-owned Property, Plant, and Equipment as a
Percentage of Total Foreign-owned, New York State, 1981–1988

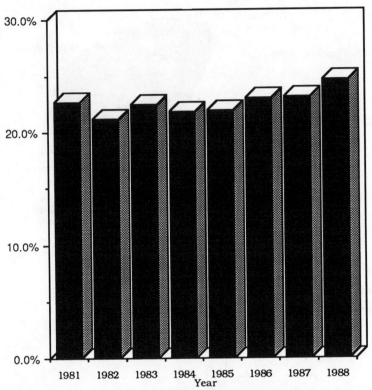

Source: U.S. Department of Commerce,
Bureau of Economic Analysis

FIGURE 9
Book Value of Canadian-owned Property, Plant, and Equipment in
New York State, 1981–1988

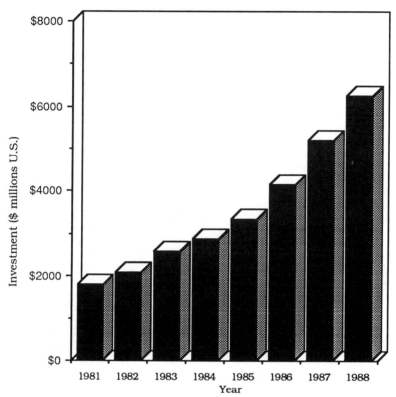

Source: U.S. Department of Commerce,
Bureau of Economic Analysis

FIGURE 10
Book Value of Total Foreign-owned and Canadian-owned Property,
Plant, and Equipment in New York State, 1981–1988

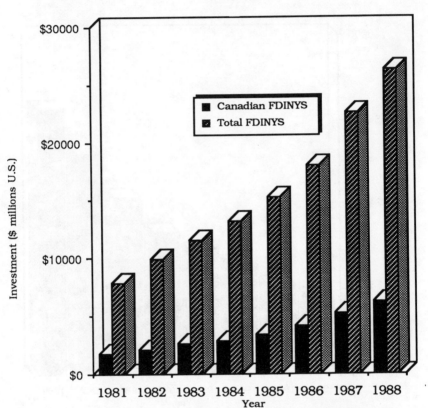

Source: U.S. Department of Commerce,
Bureau of Economic Analysis

FIGURE 11
Number of Canadian-owned Affiliates with Property, Plant, and
Equipment in New York State, 1981–1988

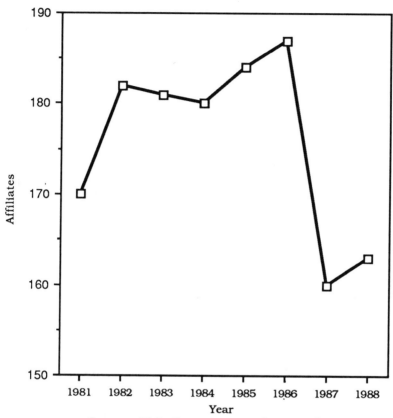

Source: U.S. Department of Commerce,
Bureau of Economic Analysis

FIGURE 12
Employment of Canadian-owned Affiliates in New York State,
1981–1988

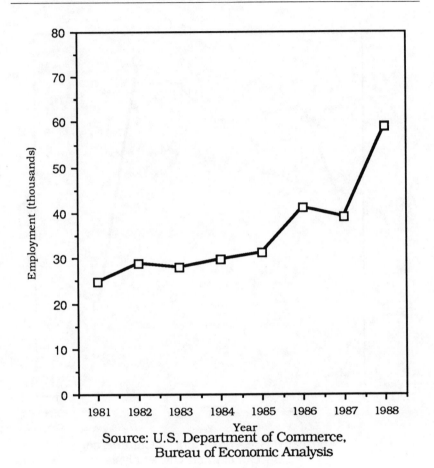

Source: U.S. Department of Commerce,
Bureau of Economic Analysis

PART III

BUSINESS STRATEGIES IN A CHANGING ECONOMIC ENVIRONMENT

9

PIERRE S. PETTIGREW _____

Free Trade: A Challenge for Canada's Industrial Heartland

I will begin with a few general observations to emphasize the close connection between Canada and the United States over the last century. The two countries can truly be said to be the best friends one can find anywhere in the world. They have been sharing the North American continent for several centuries. Immigration has been a key factor in population growth in both countries. Both countries have a similar kind of pluralistic liberal democratic system. Through North American Air Defense (NORAD), Canada and the United States share the task of defending this continent and, through NATO, share in the defense of our allies. The two countries already have the largest bilateral trade relationship of any two nations on earth. Ontario alone is a larger trading partner of the United States than Japan.

Free trade—the result of the Canada–U.S. Free Trade Agreement (FTA)—cannot be perceived as a revolution. Rather, it accelerates the continuing process of trade liberalization that has been evolving for a number of years. Nonetheless, free trade is one more spark of turbulence in the two economies. However, it will not be as severe a shock to either country as the oil price increases of the 1970s, the huge currency fluctuations of the 1980s, recent Asian competition, or important technological developments. The great advantage of free trade is that we know precisely what will happen and when, which tariff and nontariff barriers are to be eliminated, and the timing of other changes that will result with the FTA. Thus, the transition to bilateral free trade should be a relatively smooth process.

Magnificent economic opportunities await us over the next few years. Because of my job as a management consultant for medium-sized manufacturing companies, I have been particularly sensitive to the challenges that free trade will present before some of the opportunities materialize.

Presently, Canadian markets are more closed than those in any other industrialized country. Canada has the highest tariffs of any industrialized country, while the American market is already the most open market. Fifty-four percent of the growth of Asia's Four Tigers (Taiwan, South Korea, Hong Kong, and Singapore) between 1980 and 1986 is attributable to their success in the U.S. market alone. The relatively protected Canadian market presents an important challenge for Canadian businesses over the next few years. Competition will be much more intense in Canada as a result of the FTA than in the United States. I believe that a number of American businesspersons have given up on Canada. It is very important that people from the United States realize that the Canadian market, at this moment very closed, is going to open dramatically.

Free trade will also be more of a challenge for Quebec and Ontario because the Canadian economy is much less productive than its neighbor. This is, in part, due to protectionism. Professor Rao of the Economic Council of Canada has concluded that, overall, the Canadian economy is 9 percent less productive than the United States (Rao, 1987). In manufacturing alone, the productivity gap between the two countries widens to 25 percent. Between 1979 and 1987, growth in U.S. manufacturing productivity averaged 3.4 percent, while the corresponding Canadian figure was only 2.2 percent. Over the same period, unit labor costs in manufacturing have climbed 5.2 percent north of the border and only 3.4 percent in the United States. Canadian manufacturers have managed to stay competitive during the 1980s only because of the depreciation of the Canadian dollar, a safety valve that may not be available in the 1990s.

Several general aspects of the business environment will be affected by the FTA in significant ways. While the technological and legal environments will not change radically, there could be a major impact on consumers, the value of the Canadian dollar, and industries located in Quebec and Ontario. The market for technology is already international. The race for economies of scale, fueled by free trade, will accelerate the introduction of advanced production methods, such as the use of automated design and robotics. Free trade will not change existing provincial or state laws in the United States or Canada, nor will it erase the border between two sovereign nations. Any Canadian business interested in capturing markets to the south will have to consider the impact on its production and marketing strategies of numerous local laws and regulations specific to each U.S. state.

The consumer will clearly be the big winner. The impact of free trade on competition will be extremely important since there will be more U.S. goods in Canadian stores. The purchasing power of the Canadian consumer will rise because of lower prices for imported products and for local products manufactured with imported components. In addition, consumers in both countries will have a wider selection of goods and services from which to choose.

Demand will likely be stimulated by price wars, causing prices to fall and resulting in more bilateral trade. However, the Canadian economy will be increasingly at the mercy of the U.S. economy. This dependency is clearly visible in the external trade figures: 57 percent of Canadian exports went to the United States in 1965, 77 percent in 1986. By 1995, the share going to the United States will likely be over 85 percent. The Canadian economy will become even more sensitive to the slightest fluctuation in the American economy, as Canada has no industrial strategy with which to challenge the United States and no diversification strategy with respect to trade with the developing countries, Europe, and Asia.

The value of the Canadian dollar in terms of the U.S. dollar constitutes a key element in the business economic environment. On the one hand, a dollar valued at $0.70 U.S. could help companies threatened by the gradual removal of trade barriers; on the other hand, a dollar valued at $0.80 U.S. could eliminate these companies. We anticipate a slight decline in the value of the Canadian dollar because of the difference in tariff levels which, once eliminated, will favor U.S. exports to Canada. The increase in Canadian imports of manufactured goods will lead to a decrease in Canada's bilateral trade surplus. It is even possible to imagine a trade deficit in view of the low world prices for raw materials.

Free trade will affect the economies of Quebec and Ontario in a variety of ways. Competition among Canadian companies will intensify within Canada. American companies will likely aim at the Ontario market since most of the large purchasing offices are located in Toronto. Ontario companies, feeling threatened by increased U.S. competition, will behave more aggressively in Quebec. This could have a major impact on Quebec businesses, as Quebec's exports to Ontario are roughly equal in importance to their exports to the entire United

States. It will be a challenge for Canadian businesses to keep Canadian clients as the east-west orientation of trade shifts more toward a north-south orientation. Companies with a cost structure that allows them to compete effectively and that demonstrate flexibility in adjusting to new market demands will perform well in a free trade context.

It is important to remember that, with freer trade and expanded markets, an evaluation of strengths and weaknesses will no longer be measured only against those of the United States, but also against those of world markets. Companies should reevaluate their strategies with respect to production, marketing, financing, and research and development. In diagnosing production, companies should consider whether their production capacity is adequate to meet a rapid rise in demand, if their production technologies are as effective as those used by their competitors, and whether the location of the plant in relation to the target market adds transportation costs which, in turn, reduce the company's ability to compete in new markets.

Marketing strategies will have to respond to new markets and acquire knowledge of potential clients, cultural differences, and purchasing power. Companies will also have to decide whether they are prepared for "shelf wars." New suppliers, some of which are large companies, will no doubt be soliciting business from the large retail chains, such as Canadian Tire and Sears. The large chains will be under pressure to eliminate existing brands and current suppliers. Canadian companies will have to adopt more aggressive merchandising approaches, placing more emphasis on packaging, labeling, and sales, as opposed to simply adjusting prices to meet the new competition. Marketing networks can be expanded by acquiring new distributors, new branch offices, new warehouses, and so on. Other firms may employ a "skimming" strategy, choosing a very small market niche that comprises a well-defined clientele, then offering a product of service geared precisely to this segment's needs.

Free trade will also mean that the financial diagnosis will be much tighter, leaving less room to maneuver. For example, it is less time-consuming, less risky, and less costly to acquire additional market share by buying out a competitor than by gradually penetrating distribution networks. However, this more aggressive approach requires a great deal of financial skill. The debt/equity ratio and the potential leverage effect will become key areas of concern. A reevaluation of the break-even point also becomes important.

Research and development efforts of Canadian companies must be reexamined. Canadian companies invest much less in research and development than their counterparts in the United States, and companies deficient in this particular area will be among those most threatened in the free trade environment.

Among the opportunities present for Quebec relative to New York State is the strengthening of Quebec's case for the sale of electricity. Because the FTA guarantees the United States proportionate access to hydroelectricity even if shortages exist, one obstacle that might have limited Canadian sales over the past few years has been eliminated. Sales of Quebec electricity will likely increase and producers and consumers together can begin fighting the nuclear and coal lobbies and working against acid rain.

It has often been said that there was greater support for free trade in Quebec than Ontario because of the larger number of subsidiaries of multinational corporations in Ontario which, it was feared, would simply close down operations under free trade. Multinational corporations account for 70 percent of the economic activity between Canada and the United States. It is true that the initial plant location decision may have been based on the need to secure market access in the face of trade barriers. However, the need to service customers, to be close to suppliers, and to accommodate local political interests, are other important reasons why multinationals will continue to produce and distribute through Canadian subsidiaries. Free trade will stimulate specialization and, where subsidiary management is solid, global mandates for a given product may very well be obtained. However, there is no reason for Ontario to fear free trade because most subsidiaries should be able to meet the challenge readily.

In my analysis, most adjustments will be undertaken by the medium-sized companies in which Quebec takes such great pride. Unlike larger companies, they do not have the means or the flexibility to adapt to a larger market and, unlike smaller firms, they cannot be content with a local market. As free trade will first and foremost affect the medium-sized companies, one can expect great shifts toward specialization and a large number of mergers and acquisitions, not only at the local level, but also between firms in the two countries.

Free trade involves more than simply buying and selling

goods across the border. With the aim of restructuring and improving productivity, the elimination of tariffs will allow for some import substitution which will render Canada more competitive both locally and in the world marketplace. The St. Lawrence valley region should seize this opportunity to develop a new sense of cooperation, possibly across the border. For example, joint ventures in tourism might be developed to encourage visitors from greater distances to visit the region.

Free trade will also have a major impact on labor-management relations in Canada as companies are forced to cut costs in order to compete more effectively. In 1987, 38 percent of the labor force in Canada was unionized, more than double the 17 percent rate in the United States. Labor-management relations can be expected to move more in the direction of the "rough-and-tumble" approach seen in the United States.

Business relations with government will also be challenged and Canadians' optimistic view of government intervention may change. The FTA calls for harmonization of a number of laws and programs that will affect the Canadian way of doing business. The ability to subsidize firms will be constrained, especially if ongoing bilateral negotiations successfully conclude a subsidies code. Lastly, businesses can be expected to put strong pressure on the federal and provincial governments to help them compete by not imposing on them a heavier fiscal burden than their U.S. counterparts must bear.

Four industries—automobiles, furniture, printing, and financial services—serve as examples of adjustment prospects under the FTA. Opportunities will be unchanged in the Ontario auto industry because the FTA has recognized most of the 1965 Auto Pact. The auto plants in Ontario are certainly very productive and competitive and should not be closed. A number of them are even more competitive than plants on the U.S. side of the border. However, the industry will witness the loss of some jobs as six European and Japanese auto firms will lose the export-based duty remission which they presently enjoy in return for manufacturing or buying parts in Canada and exporting a portion to the United States.

Some sectors will find it very difficult to adjust because of the productivity gap mentioned above; however, there is never a simple truth in any sector, even the most vulnerable ones. As an example, one cannot simply say that the furniture industry in Canada is doomed, as some observers have suggested. A particular company which decides to adjust can still be very productive. On the whole, however, the furniture industry in Canada is in trouble; it is about 40 percent less productive than in the United States. More specifically, residential furniture producers, mostly based in Quebec, are in trouble. They face a zero growth rate over the next few years and will be losing a 15 percent tariff protection over the next five years. Medium-sized companies in this industry will be quite affected and there will likely be a loss of jobs.

However, consider the Ontario furniture industry, which mostly produces office furniture. Unlike residential furniture which relies on east-west trade, Ontario producers are oriented north-south. They have invested heavily and expect 6 percent annual growth because of the expanding service sector. I believe that the Ontario office furniture industry is going to benefit a great deal from free trade. Thus, adjustment will vary from province to province and from firm to firm within each industry.

The printing industry links manufacturing and service sectors. The majority of Canadian printers are concentrated in areas with high population densities, notably Ontario and Quebec. Tariffs on commercial printing products will be eliminated in equal phases over the next five years, enhancing the U.S. printing industry's competitive advantage. U.S. printers have invested more heavily in the use of specialized equipment. Customer service will, however, ease the international competitive pressures. Quebec firms will continue to benefit from the natural barrier of the French language. Our estimates are that mid-sized printing businesses will suffer the most, losing about 5 percent of the industry's jobs.

The impact of the FTA on the financial services sector is ambiguous. The agreement allows for the removal of all limits on U.S. banks operating in Canada and exempts the United States from the 16 percent ceiling on Canadian bank assets that foreigners are permitted to hold. Banks from the United States will be free to open branches across Canada. If U.S. investors want to purchase large banks or federally chartered insurance companies and trust companies, they must abide by the same laws governing their Canadian counterparts. Furthermore, U.S. banks can enjoy the same diversification opportunities as Canadian banks resulting from the deregulation of the Canadian financial services sector. Because the U.S. financial system has not yet undergone the same deregulatory changes as its Canadian counterpart, more limitations remain

on Canadian banks operating in the United States than on
U.S. banks operating in Canada. Until the Glass-Steagall Act is
amended, the FTA's provisions create unequal access between
the two countries in the financial sector.

It is quite important that Canadians understand that in
order to meet new economic opportunities, they will have to
face an adjustment period that might be difficult in a number
of sectors. Firms in Quebec and Ontario, Canada's industrial
heartland, should be developing strategies to meet increased
competition. If they continue at their present productivity
growth rate, the future will indeed be very dim. The challenge
is there, and I believe there is no choice if Canadians want to
maintain their standard of living. Global competitiveness is
essential. It has to start somewhere, and I believe that, as far
as Quebec and Ontario are concerned, it has to start in the St.
Lawrence valley region. It is only by competing in North America that Canadian companies stand a chance of competing
throughout the world. The free trade debate in Canada has
raised awareness of international economic realities and
underscores the need for rationalization and specialization, the
keys to tomorrow's economic prosperity.

10

RAYMOND D. GLADU, J. A. CRAIG, AND JOHN T. MCLENNAN

Perspectives of Multinational Business Firms

RAYMOND D. GLADU

My approach to the Canada–U.S. Free Trade Agreement (FTA) is mainly from the viewpoint of the service sector, specifically the consulting engineering industry that is engaged in large capital-investment projects. This business is what you might call "highly people-oriented." To take part in design projects, a company must establish a close rapport with the client or have a local presence. Large projects take years to develop; the sooner and the more closely a firm is involved in conceptualization, the better its competitive chances. Once a contract is signed, it is people that carry out the project.

At the same time, since these characteristics apply to many other industries in the service sector, I would expect many of the same issues to arise and many of the challenges faced to be somewhat similar. I will refer to two or three main features of the agreement which I will try to relate to the consulting engineering industry in order to anticipate what is likely to happen to different types of firms within a more integrated market.

The principle of national treatment, a significant component of the FTA, is of utmost importance. Applied to services, it means that both Canadian and American providers of services covered in the agreement will be treated the same in both countries. There are no obligations to harmonize, yet there is to be no discrimination.

A key impediment on both sides of the border has been the requirements for professional qualifications, such as licensing and registration. However, these legal requirements are under provincial and state jurisdiction, not federal jurisdiction. They must be satisfied equally by each party within its own country, as their stated intent is to ensure the maintenance of professional standards. In practice, however, licensure requirements can create interprovincial and interstate restrictions to trade and to the mobility of resources. This is certainly the case in

Canada. Many people think that this issue needs to be tackled first within each country. After all, how can a company expect to be internationally competitive if it cannot compete squarely within its own national market? In Canada, a committee of ministers was created in November 1987 to study interprovincial barriers and it is my understanding that progress has been made.

Sectoral annexes to the agreement clarify obligations relating to three service sectors, including architecture. The Canadian and American consulting engineering associations have initiated actions to obtain similar consideration, and they have signed a memorandum of understanding to address the relevant issues. Work is progressing well. Other service sectors may follow this pattern as they come to grips with the agreement and what it means for their business.

Another important and perennial issue pertains to work permits and visa restrictions. These requirements, applied at the federal government level in each country, have served as important nontariff barriers. Therefore, a key chapter of the agreement for consulting engineers is Chapter 15, which deals with temporary entry for businesspersons. Entry procedures are to be quick and simple under the FTA. As described earlier, the nature of our business requires the presence of personnel at clients' offices at various stages of project development or execution. There is no doubt that the new measures in the FTA will ensure freer movement of professionals and business people across the border, thus removing a long-standing and highly visible impediment to trade.

What does the FTA mean for the consulting engineering industry? First, we must realize that a blanket assessment is really not possible. The FTA will obviously have different significance to different types and sizes of firms. We can, however, try to relate this impact to the structure of the industry as it is currently evolving. An educated guess is that three broad segments of the industry will emerge. At the top of the scale, in size and volume of business, are the large multidisciplinary engineer-constructors. These firms will integrate a broad range of capabilities including project management, selected technologies, and operating know-how. They will be able to generate more innovative project financing and to take equity in projects. Next are the medium-sized firms which provide specialized services of technology, possibly establishing themselves in a market niche or becoming relatively sophisticated firms concentrating on the regional public works and industrial sectors. Finally, there are the very small firms that provide either traditional engineering services to a local market or a highly specialized technology to selected clients.

We should also bear in mind that there is no "global" market in consulting engineering. The United States is definitely made up of regional markets. The northeastern states themselves represent a series of regional markets. Furthermore, large capital projects are typically designed to meet a unique set of circumstances.

Certain scenarios may take shape for consulting engineers, in particular Canadians. The larger firms will continue to diversify both in their engineering-construction capabilities and in expanding their interest in other industries. Increased penetration of the United States market will continue to be achieved by Canadian firms through acquisitions and joint ventures. The medium-sized firms are likely to focus on regional pockets or the provision of specialized technology in market niches. Their behavior vis-a-vis the U.S. market is not likely to differ from the way they approach projects in other regions of Canada. Small firms should continue to be locally oriented for the same reasons—little interest, lack of management and financial resources—as they remain very close to their territory. The more aggressive ones, those providing a unique service, should be able to venture more easily into the bordering states.

The industry structure is slightly different in the United States where consulting engineering firms are more closely linked to architectural firms. However, their expected behavior in adjacent markets should not be too different from that of their Canadian counterparts. There could be increased takeover activity of small to medium-sized Canadian firms by U.S. firms wanting to reach a regional or specialized market or to take part in a large capital project.

It seems to me that large U.S. firms are likely to reactivate aggressively their interest in large energy and resource development projects in Canada, should such projects be put back on the drawing boards. Judging from recent announcements, it seems that some of these projects may proceed. This could mean a return to the competitive situation of the 1970s, when the Canadian federal government set up industrial benefit policies to provide Canadian-owned consulting engineering firms with a reasonable opportunity to compete in their own markets. It was necessary to have these policies simply because

American ownership prevailed in Canada's resources sector and engineers' links with clients in the United States seemed very easily extended to Canada.

For all practical purposes, these policies have been dismantled by the current government over the past year, and many people consider that this was done without any compensating gain. As a consequence, if the Canadian-owned firms that previously benefited from these programs have not been able to build up the necessary competitive skills, including strong links to clients, they could stand to lose under the FTA. But apart from these major projects and other projects in the industrial sectors where strong U.S. corporate networks exist or product rationalization could occur, we should not expect our smaller regional markets to generate much interest among U.S. firms.

In conclusion, there is no doubt that the Canada–U.S. Free Trade Agreement represents a significant achievement. In principle, freer trade will lead to more economic and commercial exchanges between our countries and among the different regions. Consulting engineers are at the forefront of capital projects; therefore, increased trade and the resulting new business investment should have substantial impact on the performance of consulting engineering firms. Freer trade should prompt firms—certainly Canadian firms—to sharpen their competitive skills and tackle new fields and market opportunities.

In any case, the status quo is not an option. Increased market penetration will force us all to compete in our own backyards and in our competitors' backyards. In the short term, major changes in market penetration by competitors in either country are not likely to result. United States firms have been operating in Canada, and Canadian firms have learned to penetrate U.S. markets by seizing existing opportunities. Some existing irritants will be softened or removed by the agreement, but overriding factors, such as the overall state of the market and competitive exchange rates, will continue to dictate basic trends. The Canada–U.S. Free Trade Agreement is but one step on the road to increased exchange and access between our two countries, and innovative and aggressive firms on both sides of the border stand to gain from a more open marketplace.

J. A. CRAIG

A *Newsweek* article recently stated that by the end of 1989 there will be more intelligence, measured in information processing capability, in the world's inventory of desktop personal computers (PCs) than in all the mainframes shipped by all the manufacturers since the invention of the computer. That in itself is a striking assessment. But another striking estimate is that the average PC today is being utilized at merely 3 to 8 percent of its potential, while the utilization of mainframe computing power generally runs to about 99.9 percent. These figures are important signposts on the road to the economic future for every region in North America and indeed around the globe.

I would like to share some thoughts about the environment for trade in information goods and services from my perspective as an executive with Bell Northern Research and with Northern Telecom. Northern Telecom is the second largest telecommunications systems manufacturer in North America and the world leader in the field of digital telecommunications with systems in service in over 70 nations. Freer Canada–U.S. trade presents specific opportunities for companies, entrepreneurs, and their supporting government decision makers in the telecommunications industry. I will highlight some of these opportunities below.

Business operates today in what has truly become an information age. This term reflects the fact that the ability to access, manipulate, and disseminate information—data, text, and voice—has become a fundamental building block for corporate and organizational productivity and success. The need to enhance information management capability represents perhaps the most dramatic source of economic opportunity today. Knowledge, which really is organized information, is truly wealth creating. Moreover, the focus of the opportunity lies not in "high-tech" hardware, but in networking and, in particular, networking-applications software that will unleash the potential of the PC in the office, classroom, and home.

From the perspective of a multinational information-technology corporation, one of the most important observations I can make is that the move towards freer trade between the United States and Canada represents more a ripple of advance than a wave of discontinuity. Our two countries—the two biggest trading partners in the world—have been moving toward liberalized trade for over 40 years. The average nominal tariff on dutiable goods entering Canada is under 10 percent and over 70 percent of the goods cross the border duty free. The point is basic: while the FTA is an evolutionary step and a beneficial one, it does not, by itself, represent the guaranteed source of new advantage and success for any firm or, indeed, for any region.

What our evolving environment does guarantee is a more open and competitive marketplace, a marketplace that reflects the heightened economic competition that is a global reality. In such an environment, it is essential that small and medium-sized businesses, not simply megafirms, acquire an international mindset that looks for opportunities on a global scale and recognizes that innovative products and services must be of world-class quality. This challenge is real and unavoidable.

In an increasingly open and competitive marketplace, the product or system must excel at providing unique customer value—value greater than that of competitor systems around the world—in order to survive. Customers in today's information age cannot afford to sacrifice their own competitive ability by using technology or services that are second-rate. It is this vital need for innovative tools to enhance the competitive abilities of firms, institutions, and individuals in today's information age that is the fundamental source of exciting new opportunities.

Telecommunications is inextricably linked to economic activity and growth. The telecommunications networks in Canada and the United States have long been integrated. We have enjoyed benefits from that integration and have seen many of the opportunities it provides. Today, many new opportunities lie in innovative information services—everything from commercial data bases to telemarketing and teleshopping—and in the software that supports their delivery and use. In fact, according to computer expert Tom Forester's *High Tech Society*, the world market for software is expected to exceed $110 billion in 1990, up from only $30 billion in 1984.

What makes this opportunity so vital and exciting is not just the rapid growth in the number of PCs, estimated by the Gartner Group to reach 46 million by the year 2000. Equally important, but not widely recognized, is that we are on the threshold of a giant leap forward in the development of telecommunications networks. Emerging technology is making possible whole new dimensions of capability for individuals and organizations to access, manage, share, distribute, and manipulate information in virtually all of its forms, including voice, data, text, image, and graphics. Digital technology is the basis for this revolution of telecommunications from a mere "voice highway" to a powerful information services engine. Pioneered by Northern Telecom, digital telecommunications have transformed the telecommunications industry from a hardware-intensive one to a software-intensive network using computer-based switches.

The basic capability of digital technology is being enhanced by developments in fiber optic transmission which make it possible to carry vast amounts of information over a single piece of glass fiber. In addition, there has been the introduction of intelligent control links, known in the industry as Signaling System Seven and global Integrated Services Digital Network (ISDN) standards. These standards offer users new vehicles to control, rather than to be controlled by, the telecommunications channels that they receive in their homes and offices.

The bottom line on these technological developments is that they provide increases in information carrying capacity, user control, and data processing capability that will result in a network with enormous potential for creating and processing information, as well as transmitting it. In fact, the provision of network-based information services from processors linked directly to central office switches is already one of the fastest growing areas for database applications. For example, there are more than 100 network-based information services provided through the Bell Canada system. They provide sports highlights, winning lottery numbers, weather reports and similar types of information. We can expect many more services of greater substance and impact, such as financial data, consumer information, and entertainment, to name just a few of the more obvious ones.

In France, a network-based service called Minitel has already enjoyed considerable success. Minitel currently connects three million households and businesses to over five thousand database providers. It also offers capabilities for teleshopping and telebanking. Bell Canada and Northern Telecom introduced a pilot system in Quebec in 1988 with an enriched terminal capability offering better definition and color image for a more user-friendly system. The success of this pilot program, with over twenty thousand customers in the first nine months, is indicative of the demand for such services. This initiative also offers the software industry a superb opportunity for growth because the network provides the platform to deliver innovative information services to an extensive audience, and most of these services will be provided by small business entrepreneurs. Indeed, in 1988 the number of software-based companies in Ottawa grew by 40 percent.

What makes the potential of this network platform even more dramatic will be its future use in combination with other information technologies and software. For example, *Newsweek* recently carried a story on what has been called "hypermedia," an approach that blends personal computing, video, photography, and sound into a multi-media information program. It involves a new computer software program called "hypertext" that organizes data so that users can move easily from subject to subject without needing an index or table of contents. The article cites a number of examples where hypermedia systems are already in use, such as Stanford University, where students can move through thousands of anatomical photographs simply by moving a cursor on a computer screen. Working with these images, the student can manipulate and analyze the human body in ways not possible with a real subject.

More significantly, the telecommunications network is now capable of delivering cost-effective access to such a system not just at Stanford but almost anywhere on this continent, indeed, almost anywhere in the world. This capacity to reach mass audiences will provide new revenue opportunities for innovative software package designers and hypermedia service providers. This is just one in a universe of opportunities that will be reality in the not-so-distant future, perhaps within a year. The territory is wide open for both established software firms and the visionary entrepreneur.

The software industry can expect to capitalize on future network enrichment. Examples include network-based voice recognition, talking yellow pages, calling number identification, facsimile networking, and multi-media conferencing. Information services can have new applications in merchandising, procurement, medicine, graphic arts, and personal services. Indeed, the human mind is the only limit to what these services can provide. The sources of opportunity in information services and software are real and clear, as telecommunications networks are being opened up for the first time in over 100 years to third-party applications use. Therein lie significant opportunities for new business growth: network-based software applications utilizing the new control elements available through ISDN and Signaling System Seven coupled with new software systems such as hypertext. This potent mixture will simplify teacher-to-student, student-to-book, business-to-business, and person-to-person interactions.

That companies and enterprising individuals can provide software applications and databases that can unleash the true power of information technology represents an economic opportunity on a global scale. I truly mean global, because the control signal standards that I am talking about are, in fact, global in nature. The sole industrial infrastructure required to start a business in this area is a personal computer with access to a communications channel provided by your telephone company equipped with new control signaling. Unlike conventional manufacturing, software competitiveness is not governed by economies of scale and local natural resources, but rather by market knowledge, innovation in application, entrepreneurial drive, and talent. In other words, the opportunity is there for any region and its entrepreneurs to seize. But the advantage will go to those regions best served by advanced telecommunications services.

In conclusion, freer trade between the United States and Canada represents a natural evolution of a long-standing trend. Increased competition on a global basis is a fundamental fact of life that businesses face in today's environment. It is the development of software-based information services that represents the most important area of opportunity for any region and its companies. A specific field for exciting growth and development is the creation of applications software to support the new service capabilities coming on stream from our public and private telecommunications networks. Somewhere out there is the talent that will create the software package that will do for information networking what Visi-calc did to popularize the personal computer.

JOHN T. MCLENNAN

My comments about the Canada–U.S. Free Trade Agreement (FTA) are based on my own experience, which has been almost exclusively in launching and developing strategies for emerging companies with a focus primarily on the application of new technology. I am very biased, of course, but I think this is the most important sector of the economy. At a conference not long ago in Boston, the chief economist for First Boston Bank said, "We've created 25 or 30 million new jobs in the United States in the last 20 years." That has not happened in Japan and it has not happened in Europe. When an analysis is made, it is found that the jobs came from the new entrepreneurial growth companies, and those sorts of firms play a major role in both Canada and the United States.

My business experience in Canada can be segmented into three industries: the defense business, with Leigh Instruments; the telecommunications hardware business, with Mitel;

and the telecommunications services business, with Cantel. I
will try to examine some of the economic implications of the
Canada–U.S. Free Trade Agreement in light of my experiences
in exporting to the United States.

Canada and the United States already have a "free trade
agreement" on defense issues. It is called the U.S.–Canada
Defense Sharing Agreement. The underlying principle is that
we are jointly defending this magnificent area called North
America and, therefore, we should be able to exchange goods
and services related to the defense industry. This is not to say
that no duties or tariffs are applicable on goods traded under
that agreement, but in defense contracts, duties and tariffs
have been relatively insignificant. U.S. companies who want to
bid on Canadian defense contracts may encounter some
restrictions, such as offset requirements, but they are not pro-
hibitive. As one example, Raytheon in Massachusetts has been
awarded over $1.5 billion (Cdn.) in contracts from the Canadi-
an government in the last five years.

Mitel, the telecommunications hardware company, was one
of the three fastest growing companies in the *world* for seven
years, which is a long time in the technology business. However, it was not the Canadian marketplace that supported the
growth of Mitel. The only reason Mitel expanded as it did was
that the U.S. market was available to it. The Canadian
telecommunications market is just now beginning to open up,
but the telecommunications market has been open in the United States since 1968. That was when the "Carter Phone Decision" allowed interconnection to the telephone network of
equipment other than the telephone company's own equipment. It was the opportunity we needed at Mitel because we
had developed the very best small PBX telephone system in the
world. Once the market opened up, we were able to grow very
rapidly around the world.

Duties and tariffs were something to consider at the time.
For instance, when we wanted to manufacture products in
Canada and ship them to the United States, we had to import
many of the components from the United States. Of course, we
paid duty on those components. When we later assembled our
products and shipped them back, we were able to retrieve that
duty through a duty-drawback mechanism. Even if the FTA
only does away with the duties and drawbacks, it will be an
enormous advantage for all companies in Canada.

When Mitel began expanding very rapidly, the first factory

we built outside Canada was in Ogdensburg, New York. This decision was not based on tariffs or duties, but on the fact that on many occasions we had to be able to say that we were a U.S.-based company. In 1983, British Telecom acquired Mitel and it began closing factories. Factories have closed in Boca Raton and Puerto Rico, but not in Ogdensburg, New York. In fact, the Mitel facility in Ogdensburg employs 300 to 400 people, making it a very important member of the local business community.

Since the early 1980s there have been many new, exciting companies started in Ottawa. One of the cofounders of Mitel is already in his third year of business with a company based totally on technology conceived at Mitel, and that company's sales exceeded $70 million (Cdn.) in 1988. The success of this company has nothing to do with duties and tariffs, however. It is successful because it produces the highest quality product of its type in the world, and that is really how technology companies survive.

The third company, Cantel, is a telecommunications service business in Canada. It was awarded a license to offer cellular telecommunications service across Canada in competition with the telephone company. Telephone companies in Canada still enjoy a monopoly and the country has one of the finest telephone systems in the world. Cantel was not operating within an industry that was competitive in the world marketplace; it was dealing strictly with the Canadian market. Since no foreigners are allowed to own more than 20 percent of a Canadian company in telecommunications service, it is a protected market. Managing Cantel was very comfortable compared to running Mitel or companies that must compete against the Japanese, the Americans, and the other global companies. Thus, I am a little ambivalent about free trade because I understand how comfortable it can be to operate a business in a protected market.

Canada has actually determined that essential "fabric-building industries" cannot be owned by foreign organizations. Basic telecommunications services must be Canadian, and it will continue that way after implementation of the FTA. Our cultural industries such as the broadcasting industry are very strictly Canadian-owned. Transportation and, I hope, the beer industry will also stay Canadian. These industries are essential to the fiber of the country. Companies that are protected and isolated from real world conditions in order to protect the Canadian culture and Canadian fiber are wonderful companies to manage because you can focus on just the issues in Cana-

da. They are strongly asset-based and they do nothing but
grow in a predictable environment.

In spite of all that, the emerging technology companies in
Canada supported the FTA because it assures the opportunity
to participate in the U.S. marketplace. It would be tragic if
these new companies with world-class potential did not have
the opportunity to participate in that marketplace. At present,
Canada is the only major industrialized country without guaranteed access to a market of at least 100 million people. For
us, guaranteed opportunity to participate and compete is really
the issue and it represents the promise of the Canada–U.S.
Free Trade Agreement.

11

ARPAD ABONYI _____

The Economic Climate for
Canadian Investment

The Canada–U.S. Free Trade Agreement (FTA) provides an opportunity for businesses in both countries to meet the challenge of global competition. One often overlooked effect of the FTA will be to intensify competition not just between the United States and Canada, but also between North American firms and Japanese, South Korean, Taiwanese, and other businesses which want to take advantage of this larger market. The agreement will create a highly favorable climate for investment on both sides of the border. It will stimulate emergence of new business opportunities and it will create an environment in which it will be easy to take advantage of such opportunities. In so doing, the FTA offers North American business an opportunity to improve its position vis-a-vis Asian and European competitors. Tariff changes and the new unique dispute settlement mechanisms will help firms deal flexibly with the complexity of today's trading environment.

Perhaps most significantly, the FTA also contains an explicit recognition of the interrelationship between trade and investment. It is the first major international trade agreement to do so. In fact, investment at the global level now drives trade. Capital flows today dwarf trade flows by a ratio 20 to 1 and companies are investing internationally to complement and to enhance their trade efforts. They are investing in subsidiaries located in areas of competitive advantage in order to produce for global markets. They are investing in new linkages and new forms of industrial cooperation with companies that might once have been competitors. They are committing not only capital, but also technology, production know-how, and managerial expertise to ensure the low cost and high quality that trading in the global environment demands.

Over a period of time, the FTA will eliminate all tariffs between the two countries and also will reduce some nontariff

141

barriers which are major impediments to trade. The FTA liberalizes the investment climate between the two countries, making it easier for North American investors to take advantage of new business opportunities on both sides of the border. The agreement recognizes that services are now the single largest component of North American GDP, and it provides for national treatment and right of establishment. Under these provisions, Canadian and American companies must be treated equally in both countries, and they have a right to establish operations unhindered in any part of North America.

Major changes had already taken place in the investment climate before the FTA was ratified: $8.1 billion (Cdn.) in foreign investment flowed into Canada in 1988. However, there is much more to come, since the FTA provides for significant modifications to investment restrictions in Canada. Impediments to indirect acquisitions will be eliminated entirely and review processes for direct acquisitions will take place, if at all, at much higher thresholds and ceilings.

The net effect of the FTA will be to foster new cross-border economic linkages. Raw material producers will supply directly to processors on the other side of the border. American investors will be able to locate capital more freely in Canada. Canadian manufacturers may establish direct relationships with distribution networks in the United States. Canadian and American companies will be able to enter into collaborative research and development relationships. All of these potential linkages offer new opportunities to investors.

Because much of North American industry and population is concentrated in northeastern United States and southern central Canada, cross-border business opportunities will proliferate as the barriers come down. Even without relocating, companies will be able to establish new supplier relationships with clients just across the border. For example, there will be more competition for government procurement. American companies will have access to $650 million of Canadian government work, and Canadian companies will be bidding for approximately $4 billion in U.S. government contracts. There will also be more intense competition in services and finance.

Tariff reductions will occur in a number of areas. These will be staged so that sectors such as steel and textiles, where protection is high, will have the longest time to adjust. Tariffs in some industries were to be eliminated in January 1989. Others will experience tariff reductions in five equal stages over the next five years or ten equal stages over ten years. Canadian and U.S. officials are already discussing the possibility of accelerating the tariff-reduction process in some industries.* The average remaining Canadian tariff in 1988 was about 9.5 percent, approximately twice the level as in the United States. This means that previously protected Canadian industries will have to make greater adjustments than their American competitors. On the other hand, Canadian industries that depend on products imported from the United States may find their costs substantially reduced.

The impact of tariff reductions has caused some concern, especially in Canada. In my view, three generic strategies are available to most U.S. parent firms with Canadian subsidiaries. First, these firms could shut down Canadian subsidiaries and supply Canadian markets from U.S. plants where unit labor costs are lower. Some plants located in Canada because of high tariff protection are inefficient. However, they do not necessarily have to be closed. European and Asian firms might buy these suboptimal plants to serve as bridgeheads into North America. A second possibility is that U.S. parent firms may reinvest in the subsidiary to improve productivity and lower costs in order to strengthen their competitive position in a Canadian market. This is happening already. A third strategy involves specialization, using Canadian plants to produce niche products, like Westinghouse with turbines, Pratt and Whitney with jet motors, and so on.

These adjustments within the operations of U.S. firms are part of what is called corporate restructuring, which includes both reorganization and specialization. The FTA will accelerate corporate restructuring. Traditionally, companies pursued strategies of vertical integration and diversification and created networks of satellite plants, foreign subsidiaries, suppliers of key inputs, and peripheral businesses. Such structures, however, were expensive, hard to manage, and unwieldy. They lacked the flexibility required by a competitive and fast-changing environment. Companies today are focusing on core businesses that do well. In other words, the big conglomerates of the 1960s and 1970s are evaporating. Companies are spinning off peripheral activities, in-house suppliers, inefficient plants, and unprofitable subsidiaries.

---

*Accelerated tariff cuts were implemented in 1990. (See Editors' Introduction and Postscript.)

This determination to become "lean and mean" offers investors numerous opportunities under free trade, because free trade will enhance the importance of these activities. Investors can purchase businesses and plants that are being spun off. They can invest in new supplier relationships or in companies undergoing restructuring. As part of corporate restructuring, the FTA will accelerate the transition from internal to external suppliers. The traditional vertically integrated company which tried to incorporate different functions within the company is now shedding them. Many functions are now being externalized, partly to reduce overhead. Today, as Figure 13 illustrates, companies are subcontracting many functions to external suppliers. This presents investors with new business opportunities in areas such as the auto parts supply industry in southern Ontario, or in the small high-technology firms that have been spun off from large research and development establishments such as Bell Northern Research in Ottawa.

The FTA will stimulate the emergence of many new cross-border supplier relationships, but these investment opportunities will have to be carefully analyzed. Can the new supplier deliver the product faster than existing suppliers? What is the impact of the different tax regimes in Canada and the United States? Are suppliers' goods affected by rules of origin provisions which limit the proportion of a product's value that can originate in a third country? What is the impact of exchange rates? Are suppliers' costs competitive after factoring in items such as transportation and packaging? An extremely important question in today's product-cycle framework is whether the supplier enjoys a technical advantage. If price advantage were the dominant issue, the United States trade deficit would be declining as the U.S. dollar depreciates. But Americans, like Canadians, continue to buy a lot of very expensive, high quality products that are made in foreign countries.

Investors should recognize that Canada has developed several areas of economic strength. They should not assume that American suppliers will always have an advantage. For example, Canada enjoys a human resource base of considerable achievement and versatility. Canadian workers have better educational backgrounds, lower school dropout rates, and better functional literacy than their counterparts in the United States. Other building blocks of Canadian competitiveness, as shown in Figure 14, are Canada's abundant natural resources as well as its highly developed and technologically sophisticated industries such as steel, energy, and pulp and paper. Canada's telecommunications industry is world-class. Canada is now developing new strengths in biotechnology. At the same time, Canada's financial resources are considerable. Its major chartered banks rank among the world's largest, and its institutional investors are developed and dynamic. Such Canadian strengths offer investors numerous opportunities for collaboration and cooperation.

The FTA will make it easier for investors to enter into partnership with Canadian companies. Characteristic of today's economic environment, companies everywhere are investing in new forms of industrial cooperation. These include co-marketing and co-production arrangements, strategic alliances, joint ventures, and research and development consortia. In this new environment, investors are looking for partners and Canada's recognized strengths present numerous opportunities which will be easier to exploit under FTA. What is more, partnerships in research and development or advanced technology will be easy for investors because Canada's knowledge base is highly focused geographically. More than four-fifths of Canada's industrial research and development is performed in Ontario and Quebec. Almost two-thirds of it is performed in Toronto, Montreal, and Ottawa, cities which are easily accessible from the United States.

The investment provisions of the FTA will make it easy to take advantage of the new business opportunities created by other parts of the agreement. For example, the FTA recognizes the trade-distorting effects of performance requirements and eliminates them. It raises the threshold at which direct acquisitions of Canadian enterprises are subject to review and it eliminates completely any reviews of indirect acquisitions. Though some restrictions will remain, especially in culturally sensitive industries, the FTA essentially provides national treatment for investors, and it creates a formal dispute settlement mechanism to deal with controversial questions. Investment will no longer be subject to political pressures.

The FTA's investment provisions must be seen in conjunction with a general move toward deregulation of the financial industry in both countries, a trend that carries with it yet another set of investment opportunities. The pace of deregulation is faster in Canada than in the United States. As a result, American stock brokers can now establish partnerships or subsidiaries in Canada. Restrictions on American banks have been lifted, allowing them to operate under the same rules as Canadian banks. Indeed, as a result of the FTA, U.S. banks in Canada will be treated more favorably than third-country banks. It is expected that with the eventual amendment of the Glass-Steagall Act in the United States, the American financial industry will be opened to an increased Canadian presence.

Finally, the FTA opens up new business opportunities by making it easier for investors to work on either side of the border. Eliminating red tape at border crossings will make it easier for professionals in service industries—accountants, lawyers, economists, systems analysts—to offer their skills in either country. And the FTA will improve the ability of companies to provide after-sales service to clients across the border, a feature of particular significance to technology-intensive companies.

To summarize, while the FTA opens up a host of business opportunities, it also liberalizes the climate for investment, making it easier for investors from either country to take advantage of those opportunities. Investors on both sides of the border should consider new cross-border services, new partnerships and joint ventures, the sale of technology, the creation of new businesses, new cross-border supply relationships, the acquisition of technology plants and businesses, and, ultimately, the opportunity to expand markets. All of these effects can be expected in the wake of the agreement.

The Canada–U.S. Free Trade Agreement is accelerating processes that have been taking place for a number of years in our two countries. This process is going to be challenging for the simple reason that every region will want its piece of the action. Globally, there are already nearly 6,000 cities and about 500 regions vying for international investment. There will have to be more sophisticated targeting of companies by economic development authorities if they are going to attract that investment. More than ever, investors will need to know what opportunities to look for, and they must be ready to seize them when they appear. For Canadian and U.S. firms who meet this challenge, the FTA will create a highly favorable climate for investment.

FIGURE 13
Reorganizing and Externalizing Business Operations

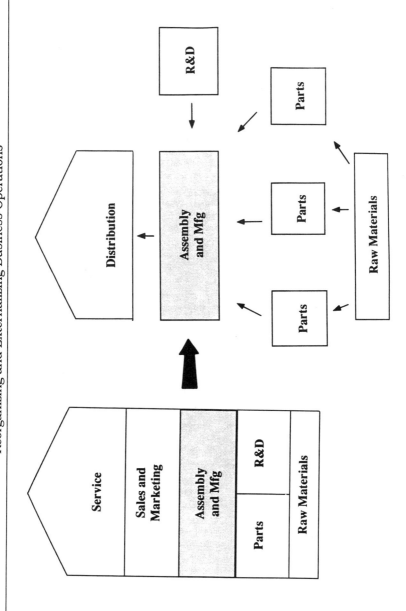

FIGURE 14

Building Blocks of Canadian Competitiveness

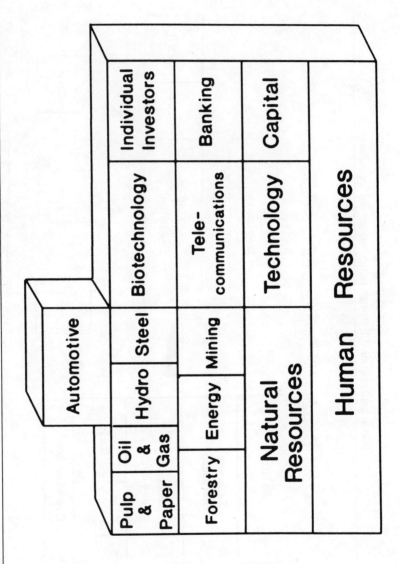

12

GORDON W. SACKS _____

Canadian Business Expansion and
U.S. Immigration Laws

My view of the Canada–U.S. Free Trade Agreement (FTA) is not particularly optimistic, especially with regard to temporary entry of business persons, the subject of FTA Chapter 15. To some extent, I agree that Chapter 15 was principally arranged as a stopgap to avoid further restrictions. But, from my perspective as one whose career has focused upon the very matter of immigrating Canadians to the United States or attempting to get them here to assist their business investments, I do not read Chapter 15 as being that advantageous at the moment. The four subdivisions of that chapter will be addressed in turn.

The first subdivision merely refers to "business visitor," or "B1" as classified under immigration law. The immigration statute under the FTA identifies approximately seven categories of business visitors. Historically, the business visitor has been a nonimmigrant who is entering the country to attend to business, typically to buy or sell products. Over the years, there were huge numbers of conflicting decisions on what constitutes a business visit. The attempt in the FTA to define seven categories may be "liberalizing," but could easily be interpreted as being exactly the opposite. Some of the people who have been admitted regularly for the purpose of conducting business in the United States or Canada may now be restricted because they do not fall within one of the new categories.

The second subdivision of business travelers creates an innovative new category of professionals, including architects and engineers, among others. It might seem from reading the statute that this category would simplify the immigration laws of the United States and Canada, but I question that interpretation. The Immigration Subcommittee of the U.S. House of Representatives, upon reviewing the intent of immigration services, very clearly states that it believes Chapter 15 was totally unnecessary. That same subcommittee identified this second category as being similar to a temporary employee in the "H1" category, which permits entry of persons such as top hockey players, people of great renown, and artists of all kinds. "H1" has been expanded in the last 10–15 years to include business managers and a very select group of executives who happen to have specialized skills. The "specialized skills" requirement has been a pitfall for many individuals who believed they could come in under that category. Under the present law, employment offices who wish entry for persons as "H1" must complete a petition requesting admission for the individual in the proper category.

The new section of Chapter 15 precludes the necessity of an application. However, implementing sections that were being examined by the House subcommittee state clearly that these persons are being allowed in only as "B1s" (business visitors). The most interesting portion of the business visitor definition is that the visitor cannot be paid directly in the United States. Thus, an architect with a large Canadian firm can be hired by an American firm to do some work, for which the American firm then pays the Canadian firm. But an architect who wants to be paid directly would be considered an employee and therefore cannot qualify.

These are the kinds of pitfalls that I find built into the law that do not seem to be carefully described in or alleviated by the FTA. However, I am in favor of the agreement. In fact, my office argued successfully for the inclusion of a third category, known as the "treaty-trader arrangement." The treaty-trader is an excellent vehicle for purposes of entry to either country, and we have never before had such an arrangement. However, the arrangement has important limitations. To qualify, the treaty-trader must be dealing in a product that is being imported. The product must not only be from Canada but, in addition, more than 50 percent ownership in the business that is being developed in the United States must be held by Canadians.

Therefore, there are limitations to the organizations that will be able to qualify under this category. To qualify under this provision, a Canadian investor will need a minimum investment of $150,000–$200,000, and the money cannot be borrowed in the United States. These are some of the reasons why I feel somewhat pessimistic concerning what Chapter 15 will give us. While some of these provisions may not affect the importation of products, they may impair cross-border investment.

The fourth portion of Chapter 15 in the FTA involves the intracompany transferee, classified as an "L1" under the immigration law. This provision really changes nothing in the United States. Canada, however, previously had a statute which required the Department of Employment to decide on a case-by-case basis whether a person should be admitted.

Although the intent of most of Chapter 15 is to avoid the necessity of preapplication for people to enter, companies must continue to petition for the right to make intracompany transfers. Under this law, the Canadian employee who happens to supervise eight or ten people cannot simply come to the United States to supervise eight or ten people here. Obviously, if this person is not going to be admitted to the United States under the FTA, Canada will not admit similar employees from the United States. The transferee must have been an executive or person with specialized knowledge or ability and must have been part of the organization for at least a year before a company can make the application. If a company is large enough to be listed on one of the stock exchanges, it will have financial statements to give to the immigration service to prove that the company is either a parent or a subsidiary of the company making the application. However, if a closely held business not traded on the exchanges wishes to open a small subsidiary in Canada or the United States, it will have to give full disclosure to the government concerning who holds the stock and how it is held. If the subsidiary company stock is not held by the parent, the company must explain how each of those shares is held to show that it is a true subsidiary.

For these reasons, I do not believe the Canada–U.S. Free Trade Agreement is quite as simple as we once thought, particularly when it comes to temporary entry and investment.

PART IV

PROSPECTS FOR THE FUTURE

13

Stephen Blank _____

Concluding Observations

I believe that four main areas discussed in the preceding pages were most interesting. First, the Canada–U.S. Free Trade Agreement (FTA) itself does not constitute a sudden revolution. While a revolution has indeed occurred and is evident in the increasing integration of the Canadian and U.S. economies, this has been happening over the last decade or perhaps longer. The trade agreement between the United States and Canada really is an effort to bring the regulatory environment in line with the changes in the economy that have already taken place.

Nevertheless, the FTA does contain major innovations. Jeffrey Schott described the agreement's impact on services. Many existing restraints will be grandfathered, but the agreement lays out a new playing field and new rules. Investment rules and dispute resolution are areas of great innovation in the FTA and will have a substantial impact not only on U.S.–Canada relations, but also on the multilateral trade negotiations in process under GATT auspices. Here the United States and Canada will go as partners and colleagues to bring new ideas to the global trading community. As Gordon Sacks suggested, problems do remain, not the least of which is immigration. We did not solve all the problems, and there is a need for new negotiations to open further opportunities for trade and investment. Finally, Arpad Abonyi emphasized that the trade agreement will bring greater foreign investment into the North American market as well as widening opportunities for Canadians and Americans.

A second set of points has to do with adjustment issues resulting from the lowering of tariffs with the FTA. Most contributors to this volume are fairly optimistic about adjustment issues, although Prem Gandhi warned that there will be losses as well as gains. Alan Rugman divided the universe into big firms and small firms and noted that the multinationals are already highly integrated. However, Rugman emphasized that

155

small firms will also benefit from the harmonization of border regulations and removal of both tariffs and nontariff barriers. Pierre Pettigrew focused on medium-sized firms and the likelihood of increased specialization, new mergers, and competitive pressures. John McLennan suggested how the new trade agreement will benefit small high-technology firms.

Though lowering tariffs is important, the agreement's fundamental importance can be seen mainly in terms of creating an environment of greater certainty and commitment by governments toward reducing intervention and regulatory restraints. Alan Rugman and others pointed out that the Canada–U.S. Free Trade Agreement is actually catching up to the activities of business. A more secure market climate will see businesses pressing forward with investment and production plans.

Perhaps most interesting of all the topics covered in the preceding pages is the regional impact, the focus of this volume. Certainly, all of the authors are convinced that the new trade agreement will have a strong regional importance. But there will also be new inter-regional economic linkages from one coast to the other. Firman Bentley looked south from Sarnia, Ontario, and said that more than 50 percent of the U.S. market is within one day's trucking distance of this region. Prem Gandhi looked north and pointed out that from New York State one can reach 70 percent of the Canadian market in one day.

The economic region of New York, western Quebec, and eastern Ontario is one of the wealthiest and most productive areas in the world. The enormous volume of trade between New York and Ontario and, to a lesser extent, with Quebec has been emphasized. Prem Gandhi told us that 50 percent of New York exports go to Canada and a vast majority of those exports go to Ontario. Richard McGahey and Jonathan Doh noted that Canada is also the largest foreign direct investor in New York State. That is why the strategic issue becomes so clear. This region already has an incredibly dense network of bilateral trade and investment, and the possibilities for growth are enormous.

Clearly, Canada and the United States are two independent countries with two distinct cultures which share one economy. We are, to a degree, trapped in our own history, but we have embarked upon an experiment of greater significance. It is significant because the greatest problem the world will face as we move into the twenty-first century is how to reconcile the increasing economic and financial integration of the world economy with the continuing existence of independent nations.

Further, it is not surprising that as we become more economically interdependent, our populations will increasingly demand reassurances that we are still culturally distinct and politically autonomous. The United States and Canada have the opportunity to begin to cope with the resolution of this great dichotomy: how to increase integration at the economic level and yet continue to maintain independent cultures and independent sovereignties. What we do together to resolve these tensions will perhaps be the most important experiment in world political economy in the last two centuries.

14

GERALD E. SHANNON _____

Looking Ahead

I will look beyond the implications of the Canada–U.S. Free Trade Agreement (FTA) to consider the future direction of trade policy and Canada's trade interests. Not too long ago, in both Canada and the United States, trade policy was seen as an archaic subject. Few thought about it and even fewer understood it. Trade policy was important, but it did not share the spotlight with monetary policy or fiscal policy. Today, trade is center stage when economic policy is discussed. Even in the United States, trade has become an everyday issue, and policy makers cannot ignore it in their deliberations.

Trade policy itself has also changed. Not too far back, the main subjects of trade policy and negotiations were tariffs and merchandise trade rules. Today, trade policy must also deal with new issues such as trade in services, intellectual property and trade-related investment measures—issues traditionally not associated with trade negotiations. I am not suggesting that other more traditional trade policy issues like agriculture, dispute settlement, and technical standards are less important or less complicated. However, the growth and dynamism of trade in services and the close linkages between trade, investment, and technology have raised the new issues to the main stage of trade discussion and negotiations.

The change in public awareness of trade and the change in focus of trade policy reflect the different world in which we now live. The world has become significantly smaller. We live in a rapidly changing, highly competitive, and increasingly interdependent world where new economic opportunities are created daily. At the same time, pressures on policy makers continue to grow. This has been clearly demonstrated in recent years by the growth of protectionism and its threat to the world trading system.

An open, middle-sized economy, Canada cannot and has not ignored what has been happening in the world economy in the areas of international trade, investment, and technology.

159

Our trade policy, especially in recent years, has been formulated as a response to the reality of this interdependent world. In some cases, Canada is taking a leading role with respect to both the old and new issues in international trade. Under the current government, we have been instructed to pursue a two-track trade policy consisting of bilateral negotiations with the United States and multilateral negotiations in the General Agreement on Tariffs and Trade (GATT). But two tracks have not meant two destinations. Both multilaterally and bilaterally, we have sought the same two basic objectives: improved and more secure access to foreign markets for our producers and improved systems to mitigate defective trade rules and settle disputes.

More specifically, our interests, goals, and priorities for both of these tracks have been to create new trade and investment opportunities through tariff reduction and to improve access to foreign markets for Canadian agricultural resources, manufactured products, and services.

There are open markets in all corners of the world to combat the rise of protectionism and the formation of discriminatory preferential trading blocks. We are encouraging newly industrialized countries to accept more balanced obligations as major traders and to grant developed countries competitive access to their markets in return for continued fair access to our markets. We are promoting international rules and trying to discipline restrictive and distorting trade practices. We are also trying to achieve proper limits and clear rules for subsidies and for the application of duties. Among other issues, we seek to improve the rules against trade-distorting subsidies, predatory pricing, and dumping, as well as to establish a better system for countering those practices. We seek comprehensive rules and proper limits for safeguards and we want to bring international trade rules up to date and develop new and effective rules for services and other new issues. Finally, and very importantly to Canada, we hope to improve the organization and the function of the GATT in cooperation with other international economic organizations.

The conclusion of the trade agreement with the United States stands as testimony that Canada is prepared to negotiate seriously on some of the most difficult trade issues before the international community. The FTA does many things. It extends the principle of national treatment between our two countries, and it provides a framework for consulting and adjudicating new trade controversies as they may arise. Important problems in the wider multilateral domain may require the same or different treatment, but they will be dealt with no less seriously on Canada's part. Many people oppose Canada making binding commitments toward the United States; these same people are prepared to risk Canada's future. Trade options in a multilateral context require similar commitments, in some cases commitments to countries much more competitive with Canada than the United States.

Canada did not enter into free trade negotiations with the United States as the result of a whim. It was a course that made sense to a lot of Canadians in the mid-1980s. During the 1970s, Canadian officials were directed to find ways to reduce our nation's vulnerability to external influences, in particular with respect to the United States. People like myself were assigned responsibility to try to reach new understandings with the European Economic Community (now the European Community) and with Japan that would increase our trade and investment flows to and from those parts of the world. For fourteen years we worked very hard to accomplish these objectives. In fact, we negotiated a contractual link with the European Community, under which we put in place a system of consultative mechanisms. We also encouraged reciprocal trade missions. In the case of Japan, we negotiated a framework agreement, under which we put in place a number of joint groups which have indeed spurred new investment and trade.

The initiatives have worked. Trade and investment with Japan and with Europe have increased substantially in the fourteen years that followed those efforts. Nonetheless, when we started the process, something in the range of 65 percent of our imports and 65 percent of our exports came from and went to the United States. At the end of fourteen years, the corresponding numbers were about 75 percent. Thus, it is my view that the negotiation of a bilateral trade agreement with the United States is the logical consequence of both economics and geography.

While we believe that the trade agreement with the United States is a major accomplishment, it does not, in our mind, replace the GATT. The FTA is consistent with our obligations to the GATT and with our objectives in the Uruguay Round. As stated in the preamble and in many of its chapters, the FTA is based on and builds on GATT principles and obligations. It also sets new benchmarks for commitments which might be taken up by GATT members in such areas as services, government procurement and technical barriers to trade.

We regard the Canada–U.S. Free Trade Agreement as both a model and a catalyst for the Uruguay Round. The FTA also strengthens Canada's hand in the Uruguay Round. Having reached agreement on many of the major issues with our principal trading partner, our negotiators should be able to assess third country offers without regard to our arrangements with the United States. We also believe the FTA will increase our attractiveness as a market for new foreign investment and enable Canadian companies to become more competitive in the wider North American market and eventually in Asia, Europe, and elsewhere.

The same goals guide our trade policy with the GATT, the United States, Europe, Asia, and all our important trading partners. To reach our goals, we recognize that concessions must be made to accept more foreign competition in our market. That is what the FTA is all about. The crucial task of economic policy is to promote economic growth. Growth and rising incomes result from taking advantage of new economic opportunities by being innovative and by being competitive.

International trade liberalization is an important vehicle for creating new economic opportunities, but also involves new challenges. Trade liberalization translates into increased capacity, enhanced competitiveness, higher incomes, and more jobs. That is why we negotiated the Canada–U.S. Free Trade Agreement and why we believe the Uruguay Round of multilateral negotiations is so important. It is also why we must enter into what has been described as the second phase of the bilateral negotiations, making another attempt to deal with the difficult issues of predatory pricing, trade-distorting subsidies, and the trade remedies associated with both of these areas.

The Uruguay Round is the largest and most complex set of trade negotiations ever held. The stakes are high, both for ourselves and for the international trading system. Creeping protectionism threatens us all. The GATT partners face the major challenge of restoring and enhancing the coherence and the integrity of the international trading system under the GATT. Should the negotiations not make progress, the nature and shape of the international trading system could be seriously threatened.

In conclusion, Canada has worked and will continue to work diligently toward building an international trading system based on improved and more secure access to global markets,

effective trade rules, and workable dispute-settlement mechanisms. We will do so because it is in our interest to do so, and it
is in the mutual interest of all trading nations to do so. The
threat of protectionism continues to grow, and all trading
nations must work to restore and enhance the integrity and efficiency of the international trading system. We will continue to
be an active and leading player in the Uruguay Round, and we
believe that the Canada–U.S. Free Trade Agreement can serve
to further the cause of trade liberalization on a global basis.

POSTSCRIPT

Assessing the impact of the Canada-U.S. Free Trade Agreement (FTA) in the autumn of 1990 is a risky task, particularly for economists. We try not to arrive at analytical conclusions or policy prescriptions on the basis of anecdotal evidence. Yet that sort of "evidence" of the FTA's impact abounds, particularly in Canadian media reports of plants being closed and workers laid off. Such reports are often accompanied by statements from labor organizations and other concerned Canadians about the damage that freer trade is doing to that country.

It is important to note that many of the trade-liberalizing measures embodied in the FTA were not introduced in their complete and final form on 1 January 1989. For example, some tariffs are to be reduced over a ten-year period; the threshold for Canadian review of U.S. acquisitions of Canadian companies is gradually being raised; and in areas like services the FTA provides for national treatment in future regulations while existing ones are grandfathered. Furthermore, even if all of the provisions of the FTA had taken effect immediately, their economic impact would be felt gradually. Another problem with early assessments of the FTA's impact is that reliable data concerning trade, investment, employment, and other measures of economic activity are only available with a considerable time lag. Even then, analysis of the economic impacts of the FTA is difficult since trade and investment activities are influenced by a host of economic and other factors, many of which have changed significantly since the FTA was implemented in early 1989.

Throughout 1989 and 1990, the Canadian economy has labored under the impact of relatively high short-term interest rates; for example, the spread between the Canadian and U.S. 3-month treasury bills reached 598 basis points in May 1990, compared to a 200 to 300 basis point spread as recently as the fall of 1988 (*Bank of Canada Review,* September, 1990). Apart from their dampening effect on domestic aggregate expenditures, the relatively high Canadian interest rates strengthened the value of the Canadian dollar, which reached a 12-year high against the U.S. dollar in the summer of 1990. While the magnitude of the effect of these factors on bilateral trade and investment may be difficult to calculate, exchange rate appreciation generally worsens the trade balance. Moreover, growth in aggregate spending in the United States has also slowed over the past year, meaning relatively less demand for imports from Canada. These factors combined to make adjustment in Canada to freer trade with the United States far more difficult than it otherwise might have been.

In this postscript we will review the available trade and investment data for 1989 and the first six months of 1990, along with other relevant indicators of bilateral trade-related activity. We also will discuss the decisions reached by the binational dispute settlement panels established by the FTA and comment more specifically on other national and regional factors likely to have an impact on the economic response to freer trade. These factors include Canadian participation in negotiations between the United States and Mexico concerning the liberalization of trade and investment, the implementation of the goods and services tax (GST) in Canada, and the future of Quebec. We conclude the postscript with some thoughts on the current status of the GATT talks.

BILATERAL TRADE AND INVESTMENT FLOWS

Trade statistics are available for 1989 and the first six months of 1990. Bilateral trade in goods increased from $157.9 billion (U.S.) in 1988 to $169.1 billion in 1989.[1] The value of merchandise exports from the United States to Canada increased by 8.4 percent from their 1988 level, while the value of imports from Canada rose by 5.9 percent. As a result, the U.S. merchandise trade deficit with Canada narrowed by $1.2 billion to $9.7 billion in 1989. Preliminary figures for the first six months of 1990 show U.S. exports to Canada 3.8 percent ahead of levels for the same period in 1989 while Canadian exports to the United States rose by only .09 percent.

The list of major exports from each country to the other shows little change from 1988 to 1989, as shown in Table 19. However, among the top ten commodity groups, export values from the United States to Canada rose for electronic computers, electronic tubes and semiconductors, other telecommunications and related equipment, and miscellaneous equipment.

The list of major bilateral Canadian exports remained virtually identical to the 1988 ranking except for the appearance of other telecommunications and related equipment. The variation in major exports from the U.S. might reflect a combination of increased Canadian spending on capital goods, the stronger purchasing power of the Canadian dollar, and tariff reductions during the FTA's first year.

Figures for the value of New York State exports to Canada are available at the two-digit Standard Industrial Classification (SIC) level. Table 20 shows New York State industries ranked according to the largest percentage increase and the largest percentage decrease in the value of exports for 1989. Also shown are industries with the highest export values for that year. Some of the industries experiencing the largest percentage increases faced relatively high Canadian tariffs in the pre-FTA period. These New York State industries, along with those experiencing the largest percentage decreases, are generally not the state's major exporters to Canada (see Part C of Table 20), perhaps reflecting the fact that most bilateral trade was duty-free before the FTA was implemented. The industries with the highest export values in 1989 are evenly split between those whose exports rose and those whose exports fell from their 1988 levels.

Investment flows between the two countries in 1989 continued trends observed earlier in the decade. The cumulative stock of U.S. direct investment in Canada, measured by year-end book values of debt and equity financing from foreign parent companies, rose 7 percent during 1989 with the largest gains in banking (21 percent) and manufacturing (12 percent). Likewise, the stock of Canadian direct investment in the United States increased by 15 percent overall, with "other industries" and manufacturing recording gains of 55 percent and 23 percent, respectively. However, measured in terms of annual capital flows, overall Canadian direct investment in the United States declined 4 percent in 1989 to $2.7 billion (U.S.), even though Canadian investment in U.S. manufacturing rose 44 percent. Annual capital outflows from the United States to Canada fell 48 percent overall from 1988 levels to $1.4 billion, at the same time that U.S. investment in Canadian manufacturing registered a hefty 386 percent increase over the 1988 period (U.S. Department of Commerce, *Survey of Current Business,* August, 1990).

Discussion of bilateral economic activity would be incomplete

without mention of border crossings, particularly travel from
Canada to the United States. More than 43 million Canadian
residents made same-day trips to the United States in 1989,
while there were just over 20 million same-day trips by U.S. residents to Canada in the same period (Statistics Canada, *International Travel*). The number of Canadians returning from the
United States rose by 19.7 percent in 1989, compared with a
16.8 percent increase during 1988. The figures for the first six
months of 1990 show an additional 19 percent increase compared to the same period in 1989. In contrast, the number of
non-residents entering Canada from the United States fell in
1988 by 4 percent, in 1989 by another 3 percent, and for the
first six months of 1990 were unchanged from a year earlier.
Persons traveling back and forth within a 24-hour period may
include, *inter alia*, tourists, shoppers, and businesspersons
temporarily visiting the other country to engage in business-
related activities. While some of the increased cross-border
travel by Canadians may be due to opportunities spurred by the
FTA, it is clear that the purchasing power of the strong Canadian dollar has also played a major role.

BILATERAL DISPUTE SETTLEMENT

The dispute settlement mechanisms set out in the FTA are
widely regarded as important innovations. Binational panels
have been constituted under provisions of both Chapter 18
and Chapter 19 and have issued findings. While it is difficult
to evaluate the success of this feature of the FTA at this point
in time, it can be said that the bilateral dispute settlement process seems to be working.[2] To date, about one percent of the
value of total bilateral trade has been subject to binational
panel review.

What has been the outcome of the process of binational
panel review? Two Chapter 18 panels have issued findings
since the FTA was implemented in January 1989. Both cases
involved fishing disputes. One finding concerned the controversy over Canadian landing requirements for West Coast
salmon and herring described in our introduction to this volume (page 28). The review panel decided that the Canadian
requirements to land fish caught in Canadian waters in Canada were legitimate conservation measures, but that Canada
could only require the landing of 80 percent of the fish, not
100 percent as the regulations required. This decision was sufficiently inconclusive that each country could claim victory

(Canada could argue that the regulation was a legitimate conservation measure; the United States found support for its position that the regulation was an unnecessary interference with trade). The panel's decision did not end the dispute. A decision by the Canada-U.S. Trade Commission established a permit system by which 20 percent of the allowable salmon and herring catch may be exported directly in 1990 (rising to 25 percent in each of the next three years). This decision is subject to review by the Commission in 1993.

The second Chapter 18 panel involved U.S. regulations concerning the minimum size of lobsters permitted for sale in the United States. This regulation was viewed by Canada as interfering with trade because Canada allows the harvest and sale of lobsters below the minimum size set in the United States. In a 3-2 decision, the bilateral panel upheld the U.S. view that the regulation is a conservation measure applicable to any lobster sold in the country and that it was not in violation of the FTA. The issue was ultimately resolved in the summer of 1990 in an agreement whereby the United States increased the minimum size requirement for Canadian lobsters sold in the United States by only 1.6 millimeters and agreed to delay any further size increases for three years. In November 1990, the Canadian government decided that there was no compelling reason why it should raise the minimum size requirement for lobsters harvested and sold in Canada.

The application of Chapter 18 to these two disputes shows that the panel decisions alone may be unable to bring closure to a complicated issue. Nevertheless, while the panels may not have directly resolved the issues, they have in each case brought an irritant to the table, clarified the problem, and facilitated ultimate resolution of the dispute.

A number of binational review panels have also been constituted under Chapter 19 of the FTA to review disputes involving countervailing and antidumping duties. The actions taken by these panels as of November 1990 are described in Table 21. Only two of the fourteen cases have involved requests for review of decisions made by Canadian authorities; in one instance, the review was terminated, while in the other case the panel is not due to report until September 1991. The other twelve panel decisions to date have involved review of the administration of U.S. trade remedy law and in all but one case, the decisions have been unanimous. Some panels have upheld U.S. Department of Commerce (DOC) determinations, while others have remanded decisions to the International Trade Commission (ITC) or DOC for recalculation of injury levels and dumping or subsidy margins. Occasionally, a panel has been disbanded as a complaint is withdrawn. Overall, the mechanism appears to be working well in its capacity as an effective review of domestic trade remedy law.

OTHER ISSUES

Numerous other issues have arisen concerning implementation of the FTA, including the following:

Accelerated tariff reductions—An indicator that freer trade is desired more quickly than the FTA allows is shown by industry requests for accelerated tariff reductions. In November 1989, both countries agreed to speed up the reductions for about 400 products representing trade worth approximately $6 billion (U.S.). These changes took effect in April 1990. A second round of accelerated tariff reductions is now underway with each country having received about 250 submissions requesting faster tariff cuts on commodities still subject to tariffs. Each country will review requests made by its industries and then enter into bilateral negotiations to determine the list subject to accelerated cuts. The final list must be approved by the Canadian Parliament and the U.S. Congress before the tariff cuts can be implemented.

Subsidies—In May 1990, the working group on subsidies and trade remedies agreed to a two-phase approach to further negotiations with substantive talks beginning after the conclusion of the Uruguay Round of GATT negotiations.

Technical standards—Tariff reductions raise the possibility that differences in technical standards (such as Underwriter's Laboratory and Canadian Safety Administration standards for electrical appliances) may be used as barriers to bilateral trade. Negotiations are underway to try to harmonize these and other technical standards so that the spirit of the FTA is not undermined. A committee on standards for plywood used in housing construction is nearing completion of its work on this issue.

Customs matters and border crossings—Negotiations to expedite customs procedures have resulted in extending the validity period for general certificates of origin from 6 months to 12 months, thereby limiting to an annual basis the bureaucratic review of the content of traded goods eligible for duty free status. In another area, in response to Canadian complaints of unnecessary border delays, an "open border" policy for meat inspection is to be introduced whereby meat and poultry products meeting domestic inspection standards will move freely across the border without additional inspection by officials of the importing country. Amendments also have been made to Chapter 15 of the FTA in an attempt to expedite temporary entry of business persons.

Binational select panel on North American automotive trade—Created under the FTA, this panel has initiated a study on the global competitiveness of the automotive industry. In addition, it has recommended that the minimum North American content of vehicles eligible for duty-free trade be raised to 60 percent from the present level of 50 percent. This recommendation, however, is highly controversial. The Canadian government has indicated that it is premature to change the rule of origin, especially in view of the ongoing study on global competitiveness in the industry.

As these issues suggest, both countries are actively engaged in working out the bugs of implementing one of the world's most comprehensive trade liberalization packages. While irritants remain on both sides of the border, a number of formal and informal mechanisms now exist to speed resolution of bilateral economic problems.

RELATED ISSUES LIKELY TO AFFECT BILATERAL TRADE AND INVESTMENT

Adjustment to the FTA cannot take place in an economic or political vacuum. In the near future, a number of other factors may have an important bearing on the adjustment of both countries to freer trade. These include the issue of Canadian participation in the upcoming trade negotiations between the United States and Mexico, the scheduled implementation of the goods and services tax (GST) in Canada, the future of Quebec, and slower economic growth on both sides of the border.

Preliminary talks are now underway among the United States, Mexico, and Canada on a possible trilateral free trade agreement, with formal negotiations likely to begin in the spring of 1991. With the United States and Mexico willing to negotiate with or without Canadian participation, the question becomes what role Canada should play. Bilateral trade between Canada and Mexico trade was less than $2 billion in 1989, compared to U.S.-Mexican trade of more than $50 billion. Canadian labor organizations have opposed participation, arguing that lower Mexican wages will make that country a more attractive location for North American manufacturing investment and that jobs will be lost in Canadian industries. This argument ignores the higher productivity of Canadian labor and also overlooks the likely outcome if Canada does not join a continental agreement. Richard Lipsey has argued that a bilateral Mexican-U.S. free trade area would put "the United States in a highly privileged position as the only country with free access to all three large, and growing, North American markets ... (The United States would) have a clear advantage in selling in either market in competition with products from the other country" (Lipsey, 1990).

If U.S. trade relations evolve in the direction of separate free trade deals with many countries—an arrangement commonly referred to as the "hub and spoke" model—then effectively the United States alone would have duty-free access to the other countries. On the other hand, a multilateral free trade arrangement in which the signatories enjoy equal access in each other's markets and share the same obligations is widely regarded as preferable. One remote possibility is to extend the FTA to include Mexico, an option that presents difficulties since the FTA was custom-made to suit the specific concerns of two countries already enjoying substantial bilateral trade and investment and whose businesspersons, for the most part, are relatively familiar with customs and procedures on both sides of the border. The FTA's dispute settlement mechanisms, in particular, might be quite cumbersome to transfer to Mexico, given its different legal history and tradition.

The greater the number of countries involved in trade negotiations, the greater the potential that individual national concerns may not be addressed. Lipsey, for one, argues that Canada should advocate a core free trade agreement (perhaps containing elements of the FTA) that other Latin American countries could sign if they so desired, along with bilateral side agreements on other concessions and adjustment periods. Regardless of which countries are at the table, it is becoming increasingly clear to Canadians that any U.S.-Mexico trade agreement is likely to significantly influence North American trade and investment flows.

The proposed goods and services tax (GST) in Canada may also have an impact on North American trade and investment activities because it represents a fundamental change in the tax climate in Canada.[3] The GST is a broadly based value-added tax that is scheduled to be implemented in January 1991 as a replacement to the federal manufacturers sales tax (FST). The rate structure for the FST varies across industries, although the standard rate is 13.5 percent of the manufacturer's sales price of goods either made in Canada or imported. Since most distribution and marketing activities are exempt from the FST, imported goods receive favorable treatment because Canadian distribution costs of these goods are not included when the FST is assessed at the border. Because the FST is applied to manufactured goods used as business inputs, it also effectively increases the relative cost of Canadian exports. While a broader range of products and services will be subject to the 7 percent GST, this tax will not apply to investment expenditures or to exports, among other commodities. The GST should encourage net exports and investment by removing the FST distortion that favored imports over Canadian-produced goods and by reducing the cost of business inputs currently subject to the FST.

Another important factor affecting the bilateral relationship is the future configuration of the Canadian confederation and, more specifically, the place of Quebec in Canada. Quebec has not signed the Constitution Act of 1982 and the most recent effort to accommodate its demands for recognition as a distinct society within Confederation failed in June 1990 with the defeat of the 1987 Constitutional Accord (the so-called Meech Lake Accord).

A commission constituted by the government of Quebec is now studying the province's political alternatives, including sovereignty, and will report in spring 1991. Concurrently, a federal commission is examining ways of maintaining national unity. Whatever the outcome, political uncertainty is now higher than a few years ago. Uncertainty adds to risk and may influence investment decisions as Canadian firms find U.S. border regions increasingly attractive for their expansion plans. Political uncertainty may affect the value of the Canadian dollar; a depreciation of the Canadian dollar would create a temporary price advantage for Canadian exports. Although it is beyond the scope of this volume to explore fully the implications of Quebec independence or the myriad forms a further devolution might take, it is nevertheless important to note its possible ramifications.

At the time of this writing, the outcome of the Uruguay Round of the multilateral trade negotiations under the auspices of the General Agreement on Tariffs and Trade (GATT) is very much in doubt. The negotiations are presently stalled over the issue of agricultural subsidies, with Canada and the United States insisting on substantial cuts which the Europeans and Japanese resist. Eleventh-hour negotiations are underway to resolve the agricultural issues and, therefore, to save other dimensions of the trade liberalization package from being scuttled. As Gerald Shannon noted in his contribution to this volume, the stakes involved in the Uruguay Round—the largest and most complex set of multilateral trade negotiations ever held—are high both for Canada and the United States and for the international trading system as a whole. Schott (1990) has argued that what is needed from the Uruguay Round to regain confidence in the global trading system is meaningful reform in three broad areas: market access for traditional products like agriculture, textiles, and government procurement; rulemaking in areas not yet subject to GATT discipline such as services and intellectual property; and other institutional reforms.

Failure to reach agreement at the multilateral level would reinforce the importance for Canada and the United States of the FTA. On the other hand, collapse of the Uruguay Round would mean, among other things, that Canadian and U.S. negotiators would have to continue their bilateral subsidy talks without benefit of formal progress in the multilateral forum. Failure of the multilateral negotiations might also indicate to citizens of both countries that the FTA itself deserves more respect than it has received to date in some circles.

CONCLUSION

It has been nearly two years since the FTA was implemented. During this period of time, trade between Canada and the United States has perhaps been affected more by changes in the exchange rate than by factors precipitated by the FTA. Nonetheless, there have been positive repercussions from several provisions of the FTA, most notably in the dispute settlement process, easier temporary entry for businesspersons, institutionalized bilateral consultation, and the accelerated tariff reductions. In addition, economic adjustments like plant expansions and closures in response to the FTA are taking place, most visibly in Canada and in the border regions of the United States. While the Canada-U.S. Free Trade Agreement will not resolve all bilateral trade issues, the early experience with it suggests that it has served to facilitate bilateral economic cooperation.

December 1990

TABLE 19

Leading Bilateral Merchandise Exports, 1989

A. Major United States Exports to Canada	Billion Canadian dollars	Percent change (1988 to 1989)
Motor vehicle parts, except engines	$11.9	10.5%
Passenger automobiles and chassis	8.2	4.7
Electronic computers	4.9	6.5
Electronic tubes and semiconductors	2.4	33.3
Trucks, truck tractors and chassis	2.4	-11.1
Other telecommunications and related equipment	2.0	11.1
Motor vehicle engines	2.0	- 4.8
Plastics materials, not shaped	1.3	8.3
Misc. equipment and tools	1.2	12.2
Aluminum, including alloys	1.2	15.4
All others	55.9	7.5
Total	93.4	

B. Major Canadian Exports to the United States	Billion Canadian dollars	Percent change (1988 to 1989)
Passenger automobiles and chassis	$15.8	- 6.0%
Motor vehicle parts, except engines	7.6	- 1.3
Trucks, truck tractors and chassis	7.2	1.4
Newsprint paper	5.4	-11.5
Crude petroleum	4.3	10.3
Softwood lumber	3.4	0.0
Wood pulp	3.1	3.3
Natural gas	3.0	3.5
Other telecommunications and related equipment	2.3	43.8
Motor vehicle engines and parts	2.2	4.4
All others	43.6	3.6
Total	97.9	

NOTE: Figures are reported for products on a customs basis; aggregate trade values shown elsewhere reflect adjustments for balance of payments purposes.

SOURCE: Statistics Canada, International Trade Division

TABLE 20
New York State Exports to Canada, 1989

A. *Industries ranked by largest*
   percent increase, 1988 to 1989

SIC		Percent change	1989 value, million U.S. dollars
9	Fishing, hunting, trapping	608.6%	$ 0.5
21	Tobacco manufactures	442.5	0.2
8	Forestry	398.0	1.2
14	Nonmetallic minerals, except fuels	90.5	4.1
91	Scrap and waste	90.2	85.3
23	Apparel and other textile products	89.0	36.1
22	Textile mill products	73.7	24.0
25	Furniture and fixtures	73.0	7.4
33	Primary metal industries	39.5	617.8
39	Misc. manufacturing industries	21.9	57.9

B. *Industries ranked by largest*
   percent decrease, 1988 to 1989

12	Coal mining	-100.0%	$ 0.0
92	Second hand goods	-92.2	0.7
10	Metal mining	- 91.1	0.4
29	Petroleum and coal products	-50.4	15.7
26	Paper and allied products	-44.2	54.9
20	Food and kindred products	-37.5	64.2
30	Rubber and misc. plastics products	-25.7	74.6
2	Agricultural production - livestock	-24.0	8.0
32	Stone, clay, and glass products	-21.8	31.4
38	Instruments and related products	-20.9	313.8

C. *Top ten industries ranked by*
   value of exports, 1989

35	Industrial machinery, computer equipment	7.1%	$765.5
36	Electronic, electric equipment	6.2	700.2
33	Primary metal industries	39.5	617.8
37	Transportation equipment	-1.2	489.4
38	Instruments and related products	-20.9	313.8
34	Fabricated metal products	-18.1	195.1
28	Chemicals and allied products	7.0	166.0
91	Scrap and waste	90.2	85.3
27	Printing and publishing	-10.2	75.9
30	Rubber and misc. plastics products	-25.7	74.6

SOURCE: New York State, Department of Economic Development

TABLE 21
Chapter 19 Review Panels

Product	Date review completed	Panel decision
Polyphase induction motors (AD, CVD) (CDA-89-1904-01)	1/90	Review terminated at request of participants due to CITT's[1] negative injury determination.
Paving parts (AD) (USA-89-1904-02	2/90	Affirmed that the parts were within the scope of the existing antidumping order.
Paving parts (AD) (USA-89-1904-03) (USA-89-1904-05)	4/90	Upheld DOC's[2] adjustment for Canadian taxes in calculation of dumping margins.
Raspberries (AD) (USA-89-1904-01)	5/90	Asked DOC to recalculate dumping margins in two cases; DOC position upheld in third case. Upon recalculation, DOC found zero and de minimus margins in the two cases.
Salted codfish (AD) (USA-89-1904-04)	12/90	Review terminated because DOC antidumping order was revoked with consent of U.S. petitioner.
Pork (CVD) (USA-89-1904-06)	9/90[3]	Upheld DOC's consideration of subsidies to swine producers as subsidies to pork producers; asked DOC to recalculate CVD margins.
Pork (Injury) (USA-89-1904-11)	8/90[3]	Asked ITC[4] to recalculate Canadian pork production and export figures and to review injury determination.
Steel rails (CVD) (USA-89-1904-07)	8/90	Remanded part of subsidy margin for recalculation which resulted in reducing the CVD rate from 112.3% to 94.57%.
Steel rails (Injury) (USA-89-1904-09/10)	9/90	Upheld ITC's affirmative determination of threat of material injury and ITC's negative determination on actual material injury.
Steel rails (AD/Algoma) (USA-89-1904-08)	10/90	Upheld DOC's use of "best information available."

TABLE 21 (cont.)

Product	Date review completed	Panel decision
Paving parts (AD) (USA-90-1904-01)	4/91[5]	Decision due reviewing final results of DOC's antidumping administrative review.
Small induction motors (Injury) (CDA-90-1904-01)	9/91[5]	Review of CITT's decicion to continue a 1985 antidumping order.

NOTES: AD: antidumping
CVD: countervailing duty
[1] Canadian International Trade Tribunal
[2] U.S. Department of Commerce
[3] Date when panel decision issued, not final completion of the review process.
[4] U.S. International Trade Commission
[5] Date when panel decision is due.

APPENDIX

Remarks of Other Distinguished Speakers

RICHARD H. GALLAGHER

This symposium had its beginnings when a delegation of northern New York leaders went to Ottawa in June of 1988 to begin a dialogue between Canadians and Americans in the St. Lawrence valley region. They agreed on an agenda to find ways to promote joint economic development in the region. The group decided to hold a subsequent meeting here at Clarkson to focus on more substantive issues, particularly on the impact of freer trade on the region, expanded to include not just the area on both sides of the St. Lawrence River, but eastern Ontario and western Quebec as well. My hope is that this symposium will signal to the larger community that people in this part of the world share a special bond, one that is based upon mutual respect for cultural and institutional differences within the region and upon recognition of substantial opportunities that can arise through cooperative efforts.

Potsdam, New York, is at the locus of a region. Traveling by auto we are two hours south and west of Montreal and Plattsburgh; four hours north and east of Buffalo and Toronto; and a little less than two hours south of Ottawa. In mapmakers' terms, we are in a strategic spot. Even the topography of the North Country suggests that trade and communications were 'meant to flow north and south. All the rivers in this region—the Raquette, the Grasse, the St. Regis, the Oswegatchie, and the Chateaugay—flow north to join the Canadian waters in the St. Lawrence River.

The discussion of free trade in this region goes back through the histories of both countries. As early as 1786, Levi Allen, brother of the famous Ethan Allen, wrote to the Canadian Governor, Lord Dorchester, proposing free trade between Canada and the independent state of Vermont. When that did not work, he came up with a better proposal. He sent the Governor General a price list for naval supplies and offered to get them for him at a 20 percent discount if he agreed to free trade. Apparently Dorchester was unimpressed, since it was 68 years later—in 1854—that the United States and Canada established a reciprocal trade agreement which was terminated by the United

179

States after only twelve years. It was not until now—two hundred and one years after Levi Allen's proposal—that leaders in both countries are finally ready to admit that trade should move freely north and south across the borders.

The Canada–U.S. Free Trade Agreement has focused attention on the importance of the economic relationship between the United States and Canada. It might be asked why the issue of "free trade"—specifically the Canada–U.S. Free Trade Agreement—is so important, given that trade between Canada and the United States is already so extensive. The agreement is important for its economic implications in both countries: most importantly, it guarantees access for Canadians to U.S. markets (and vice versa), provides greater mobility for bilateral investment, and also provides an improved climate for resolution of trade disputes between our two countries.

The Canada–U.S. Free Trade Agreement also serves a more subtle purpose. As the world becomes increasingly interdependent, the world's manufacturing markets will become more competitive and protectionist pressures will almost certainly increase. The liberalization of trade between Canada and the United States will send an important signal to the rest of the world that freer trade is preferable to protectionist policies. On the eve of a trade agreement which will be of historic importance to the world's largest trading partnership, it is significant to realize that taking a regional approach to matters of shared concern is truly possible. This symposium is offered in that spirit.

THOMAS M. T. NILES

The U.S.–Canada Free Trade Agreement, recently signed by President Reagan and Prime Minister Mulroney, is a milestone on a long journey that our two countries embarked upon in 1935, a journey that has led us to create the world's largest bilateral trading relationship. As we contemplate the future, it is, of course, important to see where we have been and to consider some of the problems that we have overcome along the way.

We began the current process of removing trade barriers between our two countries in 1935 when the United States and Canada signed a bilateral trade agreement under the Reciprocal Trade Agreement Act, the first step away from the world of protectionism symbolized by the Smoot-Hawley tariffs. Trade-liberalizing negotiations between the two countries after World War II were inconclusive, but both countries continued to be involved in multilateral negotiations in the postwar period. We moved ahead bilaterally with the automobile pact of 1965 and multilaterally within the GATT, opening our economies to the beneficial effects of competition and the enormous job-creating effects of trade.

Today, as I noted, we have the world's largest bilateral trading relationship which has brought great benefits to both countries. The importance of this trading relationship to our economy is not well understood in the United States. About 25 percent of our merchandise trade exports go to Canada. Canada depends to a much greater degree on the United States market, sending more than 75 percent of its merchandise exports to the United States.

Clearly, these two North American countries depend upon each other, and the agreement between our countries is, in a way, a recognition of that interdependence. The current agreement is, of course, but a step along the way. Additional steps will be required, and I feel sure that the mechanisms that have been built into the agreement will allow our two countries to resolve differences and move ahead on the road toward trade liberalization.

The United States and Canada have also embarked together upon a most important exercise multilaterally, the Uruguay Round of the GATT trade talks. We hope and expect that agreements reached in the Uruguay Round will complement and supplement what we have been able to accomplish bilaterally. Our experience in the postwar period demonstrates that there is no contradiction between bilateral liberalization and the multilateral GATT process. Our two countries work together bilaterally and multilaterally, and consumers and producers throughout North America benefit from the liberalized trade that results. I hope this symposium will be able to identify additional opportunities for the area in northern New York and the adjoining areas in Canada. Regional cooperation promises tremendous benefits for communities and businesses on both sides of the border.

GEORGE H. MUSGROVE

It is my pleasure to be here today to bring the greetings of the Government of Canada on behalf of Ambassador Allan Gotlieb, Canadian Ambassador in Washington, D.C. It is excellent both in terms of timing and in terms of content to begin to address the prospects and the problems and, perhaps more importantly, the opportunities that will flow from the trade agreement between our two countries. It is a matter that can begin to lend some guidance to those many people in business, governments at various levels, and academia who will be looking at these opportunities and, in some cases, at the adjustments that will have to take place in our two countries to maximize what we all agree will be a very beneficial relationship.

We are all confident that free trade is an idea that cannot be stopped, one that has developed a terrific momentum of its own. I have been impressed by the fact that cross-border economic activity has increased almost in a geometric fashion from early 1987 to late 1988. This activity suggests that the agreement between our countries has both the reality and the catalytic force which is very nearly irreversible. It is particularly pertinent that the border areas of our respective countries, areas that perhaps seem to be on the periphery of the national center and in some cases in the backwaters of national economic activity, have suddenly become central to a North American unit. The St. Lawrence valley and the Great Lakes basin are certainly now very central to a continental economy and can no longer be considered peripheral regions.

The catalytic effect can be observed from looking at just a few numbers in the Buffalo area. Over the last eighteen months no fewer than fifty Canadian companies have been established in Erie and Niagara counties. The level of truck traffic crossing the Peace Bridge in late 1988 approached 3,000 to 3,500 trucks per day and is increasing almost on a daily basis. All of this activity is before the first tariff has been cut under the FTA. The high profile of the discussion concerning the agreement has brought to the attention of businesses in both of our countries that there is a market—an economic unit on their doorstep—that they have perhaps been ignoring.

What does all of this mean? It means that there is both the fact and the catalytic event of freer trade that we are discovering each other in a much greater way. While it may well be ten years before some tariffs are eliminated, it has not been adequately noted that virtually 80 percent of existing bilateral trade is already free, and Canadian and U.S. firms perhaps have not taken as great an advantage of this as they might have.

JOHN M. ENDRIES

The prospect of our new trade agreement urges all of us to consider how we and our companies and institutions can serve to promote closer U.S. and Canadian cooperation. Today I want to look at what a few hundred business people can mean to economic growth. I want each of you to join in contributing to economic development. However, I do not want your money, I want your time. That is where most of the money goes for economic development anyway, since communications and promotion mean talking to lots of people. We talk to people all the time and we have a lot more credibility as individuals than does a brochure.

Economic development means paying experts to study important issues and make recommendations, and I don't know of any expert who can study your business better than you. I encourage each businessperson to take one idea and conduct a feasibility study. It can be a trade opportunity over the border, a new way to attract investment, a possibility to expand your business, or even a plan to save on your electric bills. Talk to your accountant, Niagara Mohawk's economic development people, use your computers and spread sheets. Even if it's a long shot, give it your best shot. Call a friend or an associate and get them to do the same thing.

By attending this symposium you have demonstrated your desire to learn and to put what you learn to work creating new opportunities. That is worth something. I happen to think it is worth a great deal, because anyone familiar with economic development knows that real business growth does not typically come from big flashy deals. It comes as the cumulative result of many decisions by many individuals who share a common sense of confidence in the future of U.S.–Canadian economic growth and trade. That is why we are here today and why Niagara Mohawk is proud to sponsor this conference.

FRANK A. AUGSBURY, JR.

I have had the privilege of being associated with Clarkson University for many years and am pleased to have been helpful in creating its Center for Canadian–U.S. Business Studies. Having lived occasionally in Canada and conducted business there for over 30 years, I have always maintained a great interest in fostering closer Canadian–American relations. The Canadian–American Affairs Committee of the Adirondack North Country Association, which I chair, hopes to foster cooperation in the following areas:

- regional economic development on both sides of the border;
- scientific research and development along the lines of the excellent cooperative effort to bring the superconducting supercollider to northern New York;
- cultural exchange in the performing arts;
- educational and health issues including youth at risk and family development;
- environmental concerns in the region including Great Lakes issues and acid rain; and
- transportation issues including a regional airport and a rooftop highway joining interstates 81 and 87.

It is our hope to establish a unique relationship in northern New York with eastern Ontario and western Quebec to work very closely together in order to develop our region in all of the various aspects which I have mentioned, as well as many others which will prove to be of great mutual benefit.

H. GRAHAM JONES

My particular job is to focus your attention on the word *technology* in our title* and to persuade you that whenever we consider trade and industry in an economy, it is the timely application of new technology that unlocks the door to real prosperity. If you look at the most prosperous regions of our country and our world, you will find that they are distinguished in great measure by a confluence of people, ideas, capital, and support services which cause the introduction of new and better technologies into our products and processes in great profusion and at a steady but relentless pace.

---

*The title of the symposium was, "Trade and Technology: Economic Opportunities with Freer Trade."

What can we do to generate the magic right here in the St. Lawrence valley? I will offer a five-point program. First, stimulate the creation of new technologies here in the region. Interest the faculty of our great universities in the real problems of industry. Expose our industrialists to the most recent progress in modern science. Attract more bright young minds, by whatever means are available, to this region and stimulate technical creativity right here. Second, stimulate the birth and growth of new companies—companies where there is no bureaucracy; companies where new ideas can flow freely; companies where risks must be taken; companies where, with more being ventured, more can be gained. Third, stimulate the modernization of established industry. If we are able to modernize now while the economy is healthy, we may better survive when times get harder. Fourth, prepare the new generation of scientists and engineers and inspire in them the excitement and the wonder of our technical world. Ensure that they are better prepared then they recently have been and ensure better representation from women and minorities to swell their ranks. Fifth and last, bring science and technology out of the closet and into the public dialogue. Let us find a way to bring public visibility to our truly creative technical people and bring them into the mainstream and identify with them.

While that last point is somewhat rhetorical, my first four points are being strongly pursued by New York State government and largely spearheaded by the agency which I represent, the Science and Technology Foundation. We have also been working closely with our counterparts in Quebec and Ontario and have launched some new activities with them. We have made a start, but much remains to be done.

Stan Lundine

Because of the international character of this convocation, my remarks will be focused on international opportunities. In recent years we have witnessed an internationalization of our economy. High speed telecommunications and advanced technology have allowed firms to expand into previously uncharted territories in overseas markets.

All over the world, barriers to the exchange of capital and technology are falling. The other day the first thing I heard on the radio was that a company in Silver Creek, New York, was moving to Singapore. It is what is commonly referred to as a "high-tech" company and has been involved in the U.S. space program. The next thing I heard on the radio was the daily change in the dollar-yen relationship. Both news items are an indication of the pace of global activities. Technology is transportable from Silver Creek to Singapore. We might be the richest state in what still is the richest country in the world, but our capital is transportable all over the world.

In 1992, the Europeans are going to have an even stronger common market. The United States has ratified a free trade agreement with Canada that I frankly hope will be the first step towards an American common market which will open new opportunities in both North and South America. We must develop a strategy here in New York State to take advantage of the opportunities in this global economy. As my example indicates, technology and capital can be readily transported. Ultimately, with competition our success will depend on whether our human resources are more innovative, more productive, and more capable than those anywhere in the world.

We must start with education and job training. No one knows for certain, but it has been estimated that there are 35 million illiterate adults in this country today. Let me provide an example of the problem. The president of a United Auto Workers local in Rochester told me that recently a new technology was adopted that required his entire work force to develop new skills. While he would have thought that there were no illiterate people in his union, he discovered that 20 percent of his union work force was functionally illiterate. Before computational and basic computer skills could be introduced to his workers, they had to be taught to read and write. We cannot compete if one out of every five of our adults in this country cannot read a newspaper, cannot fill out a job application, or cannot understand the warning label on a pack of cigarettes.

But education and job training are only part of the equation. We must also be leaders in research and development. Currently we have ten Centers of Advanced Technology in New York. We are following a strategy different from California and Massachusetts, states that tended to concentrate their high-technology development. One of those centers for advanced technology is here at Clarkson University. These centers are designed to commercialize the research going on at science centers all over New York State. Each has its own specialty: advanced materials, computer technology, ceramics, and biotechnology, among others. Research really is the goose that lays the golden egg, and New York State plans to do everything it can to take advantage of and work closely in cooperation with our universities, research centers, and private industries, where we have some of the most advanced research going on anywhere in the world. Large companies and small innovative companies from Long Island to the Niagara frontier, and indeed here in New York's north country, are at the cutting edge of technology.

What I have discussed so far involves partnerships within New York State. I would like also to highlight another crucial partnership: our partnership with Canada. The United States and Canada are the world's largest trading partners and a great deal of that trade occurs here in New York. It is estimated that the trade between this state and all of Canada is about $15 billion a year. Canada is New York's largest single export market. In 1987, Canadian exports to New York were $11 billion while New York exports to Canada stood at about $5 billion.

New York and Canada can benefit from bilateral ventures in technology and even in tourism. For example, we are working with Quebec on a program to try to attract more European tourists to New York and Montreal. Perhaps those visitors will stop off here in the beautiful north country. We have the people, the skills, the infrastructure, and the geographic position to take advantage of the New York–Canadian partnership and to become an area of economic revitalization in the 1990s.

The key is cooperation. I have been to Quebec and met with provincial leaders, and trips to Ontario are planned. We must find ways to maximize the mutual benefits of the Canadian–U.S. partnership. We think there is great opportunity for both sides to the mutual advantage of businesses and also for research and innovation to be done jointly.

Historically, free trade has meant opportunity. Whenever and wherever trade barriers have been lowered, economic growth has followed. I assure you that this government led by Governor Mario Cuomo will do everything we can do to set the proper business climate and to encourage innovation and partnerships between businesses, universities, federal research labs, and other facilities.

Ultimately the economy of this state and the economy of these two countries will depend not on what is done by government, but rather upon private enterprise. I am delighted that so many business leaders and people who are at what I call the "action level" in economic development are interested in the Canadian–U.S. partnership. If we in government are responsive, we will be cooperative and creative partners with you in developing sound economic development ideas. Ultimately, the economic success of this part of the state and of our neighbors to the north depends on business investment, business innovation, and the confidence that business has in the future. I know the opportunity is there, and it is up to all of us to work together to make it a reality.

George M. Brown

The Ottawa City Council, in the last three years, has done a good job of moving the focus of economic development in our city from that of a government town, which it still largely is, to more of an entrepreneurial focus. We have been able to do that because we have brought together government leadership, business leadership, and the educational people in the region, much as the Clarkson symposium has done.

In Ottawa, this partnership is beginning to show results. Sales in our business park are three years ahead of schedule. But we can do more, and I think free trade will keep us on our toes. We are just beginning to get our act together in the Ottawa–Carleton region, and now the Canada–U.S. Free Trade Agreement will prompt us to widen our horizons. I think this is good, and it is going to give us a lot to work with.

Will free trade work? Well, this year, for the first time, the Ottawa Bootleggers football team entered New York's semiprofessional Empire

Football League. My brother plays linebacker on the team. He told me that at the first meeting of the season his coach told the team that the coach of the Watertown (N.Y.) team had asked how the Canadians expected to compete in this league. The first game was played, and the Ottawa Bootleggers blew out Watertown, 37–0. Last week they won a very exciting game against Syracuse, 18–7. I do not know what that has to do with free trade, except to say that Canada can compete. The motto of the Bootleggers is, "It ain't bragging if you can do it." We have heard from Canadian companies in the United States that have done it, and can do it, and would like to do more of it in the future.

HUMPHREY TONKIN

Here in the north country of New York we are part of a geographical region that includes Ottawa, Kingston, Cornwall, and perhaps also Montreal, depending on how you define the region. We have one interesting advantage in our dealings with our neighbors that the United States as a whole does not have in its national dealings with Canada; namely, as a small region we are less economically developed than the region immediately to our north. Hence, we are perhaps less threatening. And we are perhaps more attuned than the rest of our compatriots to the sensitivities of our Canadian friends and the need to bear these sensitivities in mind as we move towards closer economic cooperation. In the United States as a whole, we tend to regard freer trade, fewer restrictions, and open borders as invariably positive. This is because, as the stronger partner, we tend to benefit directly and unequivocally from such freedom. But it is less clear for small economies and smaller cultures.

Some years ago my mother paid her first visit to the United States from Britain. She was amazed to discover that people thought she spoke with an accent. She always imagined it was the other people who spoke with accents. Here in the United States we sometimes imagine that our culture and our way of life is the natural human condition from which others deviate to a greater or lesser degree because of historical accident, bad luck or shortsightedness. Everyone else speaks, acts, takes positions with an accent. We speak purely, clearly, without guile. But in reality, of course, we all speak with accents, and the world is richer for such diversity. If free trade is to succeed, we in the United States must make a more active effort to learn about and to appreciate the culture, the political traditions, the values of Canadians, not in order to turn them into Americans, but in order to respect their valuable differences. A more wholehearted effort to do this would remove much of the Canadian opposition to free trade and make an economic opportunity also an important cultural opportunity.

Perhaps here in the north country we can lead the way. Just as some years ago Quebec felt the need to defend itself against Anglophone encroachment from the rest of Canada, so today Canada feels a certain need to defend itself against Americanism. The sentiment was basically sound then, in my opinion, and it is also basically sound now. It is up to the United States to react to these fears not with gestures to indicate their unimportance, but with an understanding of their gravity.

I hope that the next steps here will involve teaching about Canada in the schools, more participation in Canadian cultural events, more tourism, more cooperation within higher education, more collective action on the environment, and perhaps the creation of regional communication networks (including a regional newspaper covering both sides of the border) to make us feel that we belong to the same region, as we surely do. Hopefully, we will do all of this along with more economic cooperation.

As we look into the future, the prospects for freer trade will no doubt be influenced by the next administration in Washington as well as in Ottawa. While the free trade positions of the major candidates in Canada are well known, that is not the case in this country. Recently we contacted the campaign offices of both presidential candidates. In a telephone conversation, Governor Dukakis' senior issues staff informed us of the Governor's strong support of free trade. Vice President Bush stated in a letter, "Our nation's free trade policy with Canada should serve as a model for relations between trading partners around the globe." He added that he has a strong commitment to free but fair trade. Freedom and fairness: the two, of course, should go hand in hand, and I believe that this conference has helped to move them forward.

NOTES AND REFERENCES

NOTES TO FOREWORD

1. I have discussed this in more detail in another place. See Richard G. Lipsey and Murray G. Smith (1989), "The Canada–U.S. Free Trade Agreement: Special Case or Wave of the Future" in *Free Trade Areas and U.S. Trade Policy*, Jeffrey J. Schott (ed.), Institute for International Economics, Washington, D.C.

2. The lists of alleged unfavorable effects of the FTA prepared by the Council of Canadians and the Canadian Labour Congress show a willingness to blame the agreement for almost any event that might conceivably be thought undesirable. For example, listing the merger of two of Canada's three large breweries as an effect of free trade shows that opponents are apparently unwilling to be influenced by facts. Since beer is exempt from the agreement, and since the purpose is to rationalize production in the face of provincial rules requiring Canadian beer consumed in a province to be produced there, the merger is manifestly unrelated to the agreement.

3. Richard G. Lipsey and Robert A. York (1988), *Evaluating the Free Trade Deal: A Guided Tour through the Canada–U.S. Agreement*, C. D. Howe Institute, Toronto.

4. Services that are covered are listed in an Annex. All services not listed, including all social services such as hospitals and senior citizens' homes, are not covered by the agreement.

5. Management services were included as a covered service under the agreement. However, governments on both sides of the border (whether local, state, provincial, or federal) are under no compulsion to privatize the management of any of their social services; if they do decide to privatize, bids can be restricted to nationals, since government procurement of services is excluded from the agreement. Moreover, if foreign firms are allowed to bid, and are successful, they will still—by the principle of national treatment—be subject to all local laws, rules, and regulations.

NOTES TO EDITORS' INTRODUCTION

1. The Bureau of Economic Analysis (BEA) of the United States Department of Commerce collects foreign direct investment data in a number of ways. The international investment position measures the accumulated value at historical cost of debt and equity financing received by U.S. affiliates from their foreign parents. Banks and non-bank affiliates of U.S. companies are included. In contrast, BEA's quinquennial Benchmark Survey presents figures for total fixed assets (gross property, plant, and equipment) of a nonbank U.S. affiliate by country of ultimate beneficial owner (U.S. Department of Commerce, *Survey of Current Business*, July, 1989). In either case, a firm is classified as a U.S. affiliate if a foreigner owns or controls 10 percent or more of the firm's voting securities. Data on total fixed assets under foreign control is part of the financial and operating data collected by BEA at the state level and, therefore, is the measure used by McGahey and Doh in their paper in this volume. Measured by total fixed assets under the control of a foreign parent, Canadian direct investment accounted for about 21 percent of foreign investment in the United States in 1988.

2. The U.S. legislation, the *United States–Canada Free-Trade Agreement Implementation Act of 1988* (Public Law 100–449), was signed by the President on September 22, 1988. Canadian legislation is Bill C-2, an *Act to implement the Free Trade Agreement between Canada and the United States*. The text of the Canada–U.S. Free Trade Agreement is appended to the implementing legislation in both countries.

3. For an overview of the FTA, see U.S. Department of Commerce, *Summary of the U.S.–Canada Free Trade Agreement*, February 1988. For a summary of the tariff elimination schedule, see U.S. Department of Commerce, *U.S.–Canada Free Trade Agreement, Review of Tariff Removal*, March 1988. The complete schedule for removal of Canadian tariffs is contained in Annex 401.2A, and the schedule for removal of the U.S. tariffs is contained in Annex 401.2B, of the U.S.–Canada Free Trade Agreement.

4. For a complete list of products subject to accelerated tariff reduction, see Canada Department of Finance and Department of External Affairs (1989).

5. The only exception is the energy sector (the natural gas, oil, and uranium industries), where the existing review process for direct takeovers will continue to operate. Proposed acquisitions in the energy sector valued at $5 million or more will continue to be reviewed by Investment Canada. Cultural industries, of course, are excluded from all FTA provisions.

6. Chapter 18 also provides for written notice to the other party of any proposed or actual measures which might affect the operation of the FTA.

7. For additional discussion of these issues, see Hart (1989) and Morici (1990).

8. Richard Lipsey elaborates on this point in his foreword to this volume.

9. A recent study for the Institute for Research on Public Policy examined the use of federal government subsidies and assistance programs for eighty-three nonagricultural industries in both countries for the year 1984 (Bence and Smith, 1989). These programs included grants, direct loans, loan guarantees, tax expenditures, duty remissions, and, where possible, government insurance, below-cost service, government purchases or price guarantees, and price regulation. The authors concluded that only thirteen U.S. industries and eleven Canadian industries received subsidies that were greater than one percent of production costs and that "federal nonagricultural subsidies had only a marginal impact on (bilateral) trade." (p. 30) While the study by Bence and Smith is an important step in defining and documenting subsidies, it does not consider state, local, and provincial government subsidies, nor indirect subsidization through government procurement practices or such practices as the alleged use of low stumpage fees.

REFERENCES TO EDITORS' INTRODUCTION

Bence, Jean-Francois and Murray G. Smith. 1989. "Subsidies and the Trade Laws: The Canada–U.S. Dimension." In *International Economic Issues*. Ottawa: Institute for Research on Public Policy.

Canada Department of Finance. 1988. *The Canada–U.S. Free Trade Agreement: An Economic Assessment*. Ottawa.

Canada Department of Finance and Department of External Affairs. 1989. "List of Tariff Lines and Products Where Canada and the United States Have Agreed to Accelerate the Elimination of the Tariff." Ottawa: Mimeo, November 30, 1989.

Economic Council of Canada. 1988. *Managing Adjustment: Policies for Trade Sensitive Industries*. Ottawa: Minister of Supply and Services Canada.

Gandhi, Prem. 1991. "Trade and Investment Flows in New York State: Effects of the Free Trade Agreement." (Page 89 of this volume.)

Hart, Michael M. 1989. "The Future on the Table: The Continuing Negotiating Agenda under the Canada–United States Free Trade

Agreement." In Richard G. Dearden, Michael M. Hart, and Debra P. Steger. *Living with Free Trade: Canada, the Free Trade Agreement and the GATT.* Ottawa and Halifax: The Centre for Trade Policy and Law and the Institute for Research on Public Policy.

Lipsey, Richard G. 1991. "Thoughts on the Canada–U.S. Free Trade Agreement." (Page 1 of this volume.)

Lipsey, Richard G. and Robert A. York. 1988. *Evaluating the Free Trade Deal: A Guided Tour Through the Canada–U.S. Agreement.* Toronto: C. D. Howe Institute.

McGahey, Richard M. and Jonathan P. Doh. 1991. "Effects of Freer Trade on New York State: Economic Impact and Policy Considerations." (Page 101 of this volume.)

Morici, Peter. 1989. Remarks made to the Association of Canadian Studies in the United States Biennial Conference, San Francisco, November 18, 1989.

———. 1990. *Making Free Trade Work: The Canada–U.S. Agreement.* New York: Council on Foreign Relations.

Ontario Minister of Industry, Commerce, and Technology. 1988. *Ontario, Canada: L'Advantage Concurentiel.* Ottawa.

Ontario Minister of Treasury and Economics. 1987. *Ontario Statistics: 1986.* Ottawa.

Rugman, Alan M. 1991. "Adjustments by Multinational Firms to Free Trade." (Page 53 of this volume.)

———. 1987. *Outward Bound: Canadian Direct Investment in the United States.* Canadian–American Committee CAC–54. Toronto: C. D. Howe Institute.

Rugman, Alan M. and Andrew D. Anderson 1987. *Administered Protection in America.* London: Croom Helm Ltd. and New York: Methuen, Inc.

Schott, Jeffrey J. 1988. *United States–Canada Free Trade: An Evaluation of the Agreement.* Policy Analyses in International Economics #24. Washington, D.C.: Institute for International Economics.

Schott, Jeffrey J. and Murray G. Smith, eds. 1988. *The Canada–United States Free Trade Agreement: The Global Impact.* Washington, D.C.: Institute for International Economics.

Smith, Murray G. and Frank Stone, eds. 1988. *Assessing the Canada–United States Free Trade Agreement.* Halifax: Institute for Research on Public Policy.

Statistics Canada. 1988. *Canada's International Transactions in Services.* September. Ottawa.

Steger, Debra P. 1988. "An Analysis of the Dispute Settlement Provisions of the Canada–U.S. Free Trade Agreement." In Earl H. Fry and Lee H. Radebaugh. *The Canada/U.S. Free Trade Agreement.* Provo, Utah: David M. Kennedy Center for International Studies, Brigham Young University.

U.S. Department of Commerce. 1988. *U.S.–Canada Free Trade Agreement, Review of Tariff Removal.* Washington, D.C.: USGPO, March.

———. 1988. *Summary of the U.S.–Canada Free Trade Agreement.* Washington, D.C.: USGPO, February.

———. *Survey of Current Business.* Various issues.

———. 1989. "U.S. Affiliates of Foreign Companies: 1987 Benchmark Survey Results." *Survey of Current Business,* July.

Wonnacott, Paul. 1987. *The United States and Canada: the Quest for Free Trade.* Policy Analyses in International Economics #6. Washington, D.C.: Institute for International Economics.

REFERENCES TO CHAPTER 2

Crookell, Harold. 1987. "Managing Canadian Subsidiaries in a Free Trade Environment." *Sloan Management Review,* Fall: 71–76.

D'Cruz, Joseph R. and James D. Fleck. 1987. *Yankee Canadians in the Global Economy.* London: National Centre for Management Research and Development.

Economic Council of Canada. 1988. *Managing Adjustment: Policies for Trade Sensitive Industries.* Ottawa.

Gove, Tom. 1988. "Proctor and Gamble Corporate Statement of the Canada–U.S. Free Trade Agreement" by the Manager of Management Systems and Distribution.

Newall, Ted. 1988. "Stepping Out from Behind the Tariff Wall." Speech to Business Strategies and Free Trade Conference sponsored by the C.D. Howe Institute and University of Toronto, Toronto.

Porter, Michael. 1980. *Competition in Global Industries.* Cambridge: Harvard Business School Press.

Rugman, Alan M. 1981. *Inside the Multinationals: The Economics of Internal Markets.* New York: Columbia University Press.

———. 1988a. *Trade Liberalization and International Investment.* Economic Council of Canada, Discussion Paper 347. Ottawa.

————. 1988b. "A Canadian Perspective on U.S. Administered Protection" *Maine Law Review*. September.

Rugman, Alan M. and Andrew Anderson. 1987. *Administered Protection in America.* Toronto: Croom Helm Ltd. and New York: Methuen, Inc.

Rugman, Alan M. and Sheila Douglas. 1986. "The Strategic Management of Multinationals and World Product Mandating," *Canadian Public Policy*, 12 (June): 320–328.

Rugman, Alan M. and John McIlveen. 1985. *Megafirms: Strategies for Canada's Multinationals*. Toronto: Methuen.

References to Chapter 7

Gandhi, Prem. 1985. *Canadian Investment in New York State: Appalachia or a Haven for Foreign Investors*, Special Report No. 9. Albany: The Rockefeller Institute.

————. 1989. *Canadian Investment in Northern New York: Effect of Free Trade on Investment Flows*, Project No. 1084. Plattsburgh: Economic Development and Technical Assistance Center.

References to Chapter 8

Gandhi, Prem. 1986. "Foreign Direct Investment and Regional Development: The Case of Canadian Investment in New York State," In Martin Schoolman and Alvin Magid, eds. *Reindustrializing New York State.* Albany: State University of New York Press.

Harrington, James W. and David J. Barnas. 1987. "Substate Regional Employment Impact of Foreign Direct Investment." Mimeo. Buffalo: Canada–U.S. Trade Center, State University of New York at Buffalo.

References to Chapter 9

Rao, S. 1987. *U.S.–Canada Productivity Gap, Scale Economies, and the Gains from Freer Trade.* Ottawa: Economic Council of Canada.

Notes to Postscript

1. Balance of trade data for 1989 are shown in Table 2 of the Editors' Introduction.

2. See for example Winham (1990).

3. This section draws on material presented by the OECD (1990) and Slutsky (1990).

REFERENCES TO POSTSCRIPT

Bank of Canada. 1990. *Review.* September.

Department of External Affairs. 1990. "Free Trade News". Ottawa.

Lipsey, Richard G. 1990. "Canada at the U.S.-Mexico Free Trade Dance: Wallflower or Partner?" Commentary No. 20. Toronto: C. D. Howe Institute. August.

OECD. 1990. *Economic Survey of Canada.* Paris.

Schott, Jeffrey J. 1990. *Completing the Uruguay Round: A Results-Oriented Approach to the GATT Trade Negotiations.* Washington, D.C.: Institute for International Economics.

Slutsky, Samuel. 1990. "Impact of the Goods and Services Tax on Free Trade." In *Canada-U.S. Outlook,* vol. 2, no. 1. Summer. Washington, D.C.: National Planning Association.

Statistics Canada. 1989. *International Travel.* January. Ottawa.

————. 1990. *International Travel.* various issues.

U.S. Department of Commerce. *Survey of Current Business.* Various issues.

Winham, Gilbert R. 1990. "Dispute Settlement in the Canada-U.S. Free Trade Agreement." In *Canada-U.S. Outlook,* vol. 2, no. 1. Summer. Washington, D.C.: National Planning Association.

NOTES ON CONTRIBUTORS*

Arpad Abonyi is president of Prospectus Investment Strategies and Ventures, Inc., Ottawa, Ontario. He also serves as research advisor to the Canadian Chamber of Commerce in its study of Canadian competitiveness.

Frank A. Augsbury, Jr. is Chairman and CEO of the Augsbury Organization in Ogdensburg, New York.

*G. Firman Bentley** is currently Senior Vice President of NOVA Corporation, Calgary, Alberta. He serves on the Canadian government's International Trade Advisory Committee and is chairman of the Sectoral Advisory Group on International Trade (SAGIT) for Energy, Chemicals, and Petrochemicals.

Stephen Blank is Director of the Institute for U.S.–Canadian Business Studies and Professor of International Business at Pace University, New York.

George M. Brown is Alderman of the City of Ottawa, Ontario, and Councillor of the Regional Municipality of Ottawa–Carleton, Ontario.

*J. A. Craig** is currently Vice President for Integrated Network Systems at Northern Telecom, Inc. Prior to that he was Vice President for Marketing at Northern Telecom and Vice President for Corporate Development at Bell Northern Research, Ltd., Ottawa, Ontario.

Thomas A. Cronin is Special Projects Consultant for the Clinton County Area Development Corporation in Plattsburgh, New York.

Jonathan P. Doh is Coordinator, Trade Policy, New York State Department of Economic Development, Albany, New York.

John M. Endries is President of Niagara Mohawk Power Corporation, Syracuse, New York.

Richard H. Gallagher is President of Clarkson University, Potsdam, New York.

---

*Individuals whose current affiliation differs from their affiliation at the time of the symposium are noted by an asterisk (*).

Prem Gandhi is a State University of New York Distinguished Service Professor and Co-Director of the Institute of International Business Education, Research and Training at the State University of New York College at Plattsburgh, New York.

*Raymond D. Gladu** was Vice President of Marketing for SNC International Ltd., Montreal, Quebec at the time of the conference. He is currently Vice President, The Group INC Strategy and Development, Montreal.

H. Graham Jones is the Executive Director of the New York State Science and Technology Foundation, Albany, New York.

Richard G. Lipsey is Alcan Fellow of the Canadian Institute for Advanced Research and Professor of Economics at Simon Fraser University. He was previously Senior Economic Advisor, C. D. Howe Institute in Toronto and Peacock Professor of Economics at Queens University. His 1985 book with Murray Smith, *Taking the Initiative: Canada's Trade Options in a Turbulent World*, was instrumental in focusing the Canadian debate on freer trade.

Stan Lundine is Lieutenant Governor of New York State. He was the coauthor of the Omnibus Trade Bill passed by the U.S. House of Representatives in 1986 and also served on the House Science and Technology Committee.

*Richard M. McGahey** was Deputy Commissioner for Policy and Research for the New York State Department of Economic Development in Albany at the time of the conference. He is currently economic policy advisor to Senator Edward M. Kennedy (D-MA.), Washington, D.C.

*John T. McLennan** is President and CEO of BCE Mobile Communications, Inc. in St. Laurent, Quebec. Prior to this, he was Executive Vice President of the Mitel Corporation and President and Chairman of Cantel, Inc.

Fredric C. Menz is Professor of Economics and Director of the Center for Canadian–U.S. Business Studies at Clarkson University.

George H. Musgrove is Head of Consular Post and Consul, Canadian Consulate for Upstate New York, Buffalo, New York.

*Honorable Thomas M. T. Niles** was United States Ambassador to Canada from 1985 to June 1989. He is currently the U.S. Representative to the European Community.

Pierre S. Pettigrew is Vice President, Samson Belair International, Member of Deloitte, Haskins and Sells, Montreal, Quebec. He was formerly officer of the Secretariat and External Affairs, Privy Council Office, Ottawa, and chief of staff of the Office of Leader of the Official Opposition, Quebec National Assembly.

Alan M. Rugman is Professor of International Business at the University of Toronto and Research Director of the Ontario Centre for International Business. He is a member of Canada's International Trade Advisory Committee and the author of numerous books dealing with the financial, economic, and managerial aspects of multinational enterprises.

Gordon W. Sacks, a partner of Hirsch and Sacks, Buffalo, New York, served as U.S. Immigration Judge in Buffalo for eleven years.

Jeffrey J. Schott is Research Fellow at the Institute for International Economics in Washington, D.C., and Adjunct Professor of International Business Diplomacy at Georgetown University. He is the author of numerous books and policy studies on trade policy and on the Canada–U.S. Free Trade Agreement, including *The Canada–United States Free Trade Agreement: The Global Impact* (with Murray Smith).

*Gerald E. Shannon** is currently Ambassador for Multilateral Trade Negotiations, Permanent Mission of Canada, in Geneva, Switzerland. He was Deputy Minister for International Trade and Associate Under-Secretary of State for External Affairs of the Canadian government, Ottawa, Ontario, at the time of the conference.

Sarah A. Stevens is Assistant Professor of Economics at St. Lawrence University in Canton, New York.

*James R. Tarrant** is Special Negotiator for Transportation Affairs, Bureau of Economic and Business Affairs, U.S. Department of State. He was Economic Minister-Counselor, Embassy of the United States of America in Ottawa, Ontario, at the time of the conference.

*Humphrey Tonkin** is currently President of the University of Hartford, in Hartford, Connecticut. He was President of the State University of New York College at Potsdam, New York, at the time of the conference.

Daniel B. Walsh is President, Business Council of New York State, Albany, New York.

INDEX

Abonyi, Arpad, 155
accelerated tariff reductions:
    under the FTA, 4–5, 24, 143,
    174, 190
Adirondack North Country Asso-
    ciation (N.Y.), 107, 183
adjustment: under the FTA, 4,
    34–5, 55, 62, 143, 165; under
    GATT tariff reductions, 4
agricultural trade: and GATT,
    106; in the GATT negotiations,
    24, 174
agriculture: in the FTA, 6, 11, 32,
    106; supply management, 11,
    106
Alcan, 58
alcoholic beverages, 11, 22, 51,
    139, 189
Allen, Ethan, 179
Allen, Levi, 179–80
AMCA, 59
American Express, 70
Amoco, 61
Anderson, Andrew D., 30
antidumping laws, 8–9, 32, 54,
    169; continuing negotiations,
    30–1
architecture, 130
Australia-New Zealand Free
    Trade Area, 9, 52
Auto Pact (see Automotive Prod-
    ucts Agreement of 1965)
Automotive Products Agreement
    of 1965, 15, 18, 25, 26; and
    the FTA, 126
automotive trade: binational

select panel, 25, 171; Canada-
    U.S., 15, 18, 25, 126; FTA pro-
    visions, 25, 126; New York-
    Canada, 102

Baker, James, 49
Barnas, David J., 103
Bell Canada, 135
Bell Northern Research, 133
Bence, Jean-Francois, 191
Bentley, G. Firman, 156
Bethlehem Steel: countervail
    action, 55
binding arbitration, 51; in Cana-
    da-U.S. trade disputes, 28, 30
Bombardier, 59
border crossings: Canada-U.S.,
    168, 170–1
British Telecom, 139
broadcasting: exemption in the
    FTA, 22
Buffalo (N.Y.), 107, 179, 182
Business Council (New York
    State), 85
business services (see services)
business visitors: effect of FTA
    on, 26, 69, 106, 130, 146,
    149–51, 171

Canada: goods and services tax
    (GST), 172–3; major exports,
    15, 166–7; trade with United
    States, 14–16, 91–2, 166, 185;
    federal election (1988), 51–2;
    major imports, 15; debate over